MICROWAVE
COOKING CLASS
COOKBOOK

PUBLICATIONS INTERNATIONAL, LTD.

Contents

Copyright © 1983 by Publications International, Ltd.
All rights reserved.
This book may not be reproduced or quoted in whole or in part by
mimeograph or any other printed means or for presentation on radio,
television, videotape, or film without written permission from:
    Louis Weber, President
    Publications International, Ltd.
    3841 West Oakton Street
    Skokie, Illinois 60076
Permission is never granted for commercial purposes.

On the Front Cover: Chocolate-Dream Cake, Spiced Baby Carrots, and
    Sole Élégante
On the Back Cover: Coconut-Cream Dessert Dip and Herb-Buttered Corn

Library of Congress Catalog Card Number: 83-62603
ISBN: 0-88176-425-6

Cover Design: Linda Snow Shum
Cover Photography: Cy DeCosse Incorporated

Printed and bound by Pomurski Tisk.
10 9 8 7 6 5 4 3 2 1

Introduction

Microwave cooking—fast, cool, clean cooking with the ability to cook many kinds of foods and to cook them well makes this modern method of food preparation especially appealing for today's busy lifestyles. The kitchen-tested methods coupled with the delicious recipes in this cookbook will enable experienced microwave cooks as well as beginners to enjoy the advantages of microwave cooking. The clearly written, step-by-step recipes, along with hundreds of how-to photographs, ensure successful microwaving.

Following are some guidelines and tips about microwave techniques and utensils to help you learn the general do's and don'ts of microwave cooking. Many microwave methods will already be familiar to you; they have almost exact counterparts in conventional cooking. Other methods are unique to microwaving.

The first and most important step, however, is to read and become familiar with the use-and-care manual that came with your particular microwave oven. Follow the manufacturer's recommendations for such factors as power requirements, safe operating procedures, cleaning, and what foods can and cannot be microwaved.

HOW MICROWAVE OVENS WORK

Every microwave oven contains a component (the magnetron tube) that converts electrical energy into another form of energy called microwaves. These energy waves enter the oven cavity and are distributed within the cavity by a fan or "stirrer." Some ovens have a turntable to move the food through the energy waves. Microwaves cannot penetrate metal and are, therefore, reflected off the metal walls of the oven and are absorbed by the food.

Microwaves penetrate food to a depth of ¾ inch to 1½ inches. The waves cause the food molecules to vibrate rapidly; and the friction of the vibrating molecules produces heat. As with any form of cooking, this heat is carried throughout the food by means of conduction. Thus, the "outer" edges of the food—where the microwaves actually penetrate—actually cook or heat first or most quickly.

POWER SETTINGS AND WATTAGE

The recipes in this book call for various power settings for cooking, heating, reheating and defrosting foods.

Manufacturers may use different terms to indicate power settings. Check your owner's manual to compare your oven's settings to the following, which are used in our recipes: High (100%) power; Medium-High (70%) power; Medium (50%) power; Medium-Low (30%) power; and Warm (10%) power.

These power settings are based on ovens that produce 600 to 700 watts of power. If the wattage of your oven is lower (check your owner's manual), some adjustments of cooking times may be necessary. For example, an oven producing 400 to 500 watts may require an additional 30 seconds of cooking time for each minute called for in the recipe if using the same power setting; an oven that produces 500 to 600 watts may require an additional 15 seconds for each minute.

Another factor that can affect power levels of your microwave oven is the voltage (electrical current) coming into your home. Voltage fluctuates during times of heavy power usage—for example during very hot or cold weather and during early evening hours when most people are cooking. If incoming voltage is lowered, cooking times in your microwave can be longer than usual.

COOKING TIMES

The recipes in this book usually give a range of cooking time for a particular procedure, along with a description of the food at the completion of that cooking phase. Using the range given as guidelines, we suggest you begin to check for doneness at the minimum time stated. It is much easier to continue cooking for a few minutes longer than to attempt to salvage overcooked food.

As with conventional cooking, several factors can affect cooking times in microwave ovens. Consider these factors to adjust cooking times and to adapt conventional recipes:

Wattage and Voltage. See the discussion of oven wattage, voltage fluctuations and power settings above.

Temperature of Food. Foods or ingredients at room temperature cook in less time than foods taken directly from the refrigerator or freezer.

Quantity. As the amount of food to be microwaved

is increased, the time required for cooking is also increased. For example, 2 baking potatoes take longer to microwave than 1 potato; and 3 potatoes need a longer cooking time than 2 potatoes. This is especially important to remember when increasing or decreasing the size of a recipe.

Density of Food. Lighter, more porous foods cook faster than heavy, compact foods. A 3-inch dinner roll heats more quickly than a 3-inch stuffed cabbage roll. A beef roast needs more cooking time than the same quantity of ground beef.

Moisture Content. Microwaves are attracted to moisture; therefore, foods with a higher moisture content microwave more successfully. For example, a vegetable that is fresh and still retains its moisture content cooks better and in less time than an old, dried-out vegetable. (However, when cooking foods in a liquid in a microwave oven, usually less liquid is used than in conventional cooking because less evaporation takes place and there is less chance of "burning" or scorching foods.)

Shape of Foods. Thinner and smaller foods cook more quickly than thicker and larger foods. For this reason, foods of uniform thickness and shape cook more *evenly* than irregularly shaped foods. Therefore, if cooking a food like hamburgers, make all of the patties the same size and thickness so that cooking time is the same for each patty. (This is also why the thinner, less meaty parts of chicken pieces cook faster than the thicker portions. Proper arrangement of this type of food promotes even cooking. See Microwave Techniques below.)

Sugar and Fat Content. Foods or parts of foods high in fat or sugar become hot very quickly. For example, if heating a frosted donut, the sugary icing becomes very hot and melts before the donut itself is very warm.

MICROWAVE TECHNIQUES
These brief descriptions of the techniques used throughout this book will help you understand the methods of microwave cooking. With a little experience, you will be able to apply the appropriate methods when adapting your own recipes.

Arranging Foods. When microwaving foods that consist of separate pieces (such as pork chops, muffins or whole potatoes), arrange the items evenly spaced in a circular pattern so that all sides are exposed to microwaves. If using a rectangular dish, place items like pork chops or sausages toward the outer edges and corners. If pieces are not of uniform shape or thickness, such as chicken pieces, place the thicker or meatier portions toward the outside of the "circle" where they receive more microwave energy. For even

cooking, center any food or dish in the oven cavity as much as possible, whether a ring of muffins, a casserole or a beef roast.

Covering Foods. Foods are covered to prevent spatters and to hold in heat and steam, which in turn speeds cooking time. Use paper toweling to minimize spatters. (White toweling is recommended; colors may transfer to the food. Also, do not use recycled paper; it can ignite.) Use waxed paper to prevent spatters and hold in some heat and moisture. Use tighter covers—a casserole lid or microwave-safe plastic wrap—to hold in a substantial amount of heat and steam. Pull plastic wrap loosely over the cooking dish or vent the wrap to allow a little steam to escape. (Otherwise too much steam pressure can build up; casserole lids are not airtight.) To vent, simply turn wrap back at a corner or along an edge to form a small opening. Usually plastic wrap can be used if the dish or casserole does not have a lid. Remember to be careful when removing any covering; steam can cause burns.

Stirring Foods. Stir foods to distribute heat more evenly during cooking. More microwaves enter the food from the outside edges as the waves are reflected off the oven walls. Therefore, stir food from the outside edges toward the center where the food is likely to be less cooked.

Rotating a Dish. Use this technique generally for foods that cannot be stirred during cooking, for example, a lasagne casserole, a roast or a cake. To aid in more even cooking, rotate the dish ½ turn (so that the part of the dish that was in the back of the oven is moved to the front of the oven) or ¼ turn (so that the part that was at the side of the oven is moved to the front).

Rearranging Separate Items. Rearrange food pieces, such as ears of corn, sausages, individual small casseroles or chicken pieces, during cooking. Again, this technique promotes even cooking of the foods. Move items from the outside edge of a dish toward the inside of the dish; and move those at the inside toward the outside. Likewise, exchange the positions of items arranged in a circular pattern. Turn over individual pieces of food like burgers, chops or a whole chicken.

Shielding Parts of Food. Use small, individual pieces of aluminum foil to protect areas of food that are susceptable to overcooking before the remainder of the food is done. (**Caution:** Use this technique *only* if your owner's manual specifically states that foil can be used in your oven. Be sure foil does not get close to or touch oven walls; press foil firmly onto food or edge of dish so that corners or edges of foil do not act as an antenna to attract microwaves. See Microwave Utensils below.) Sensitive areas include the wing tips or top of the breastbone of a turkey or chicken. Corners of a square dish of brownies or the narrow top edge of a quick bread in a loaf dish can be shielded.

Standing Time. Some recipes in this book call for a standing time in addition to the cooking time; standing time is important and should not be disregarded because certain foods continue to cook after they are removed from the oven. If standing time is indicated in the recipe, allow for it. Some foods may appear undercooked, but will complete cooking during standing time.

MICROWAVE UTENSILS

A key to successful microwave cooking is using the appropriate utensils. Usually a dish or measuring utensil made of conventional oven-proof glass, ceramic or pottery is also safe for use in microwave ovens. Utensils made of these materials specifically for microwave ovens (including browning dishes) are, of course, appropriate. Paper plates and toweling can be used for brief periods of microwaving, such as heating a sandwich or a single piece of chicken or cooking a strip of bacon. (**Caution:** Do not use paper products that are recycled or contain nylon; these may ignite during cooking.)

Plastic utensils vary greatly in the quality and consistency of materials. Those made especially for use in microwave ovens, for example, roasting racks and microwave thermometers, are safe to use. Heavy-duty freezer bags and cooking bags work very well, as does plastic wrap. However, lighter weight food storage bags and containers are only appropriate for very brief heating or defrosting in the microwave.

We strongly recommend following the manufacturer's guidelines for using a product as a utensil in your microwave oven, whether it be a plastic wrap, measuring cup, casserole or plate. Be sure the manufacturer states the product is microwave-safe and note whether it is safe for prolonged use or only for brief microwaving tasks.

The size and shape of a utensil is also a factor to consider when cooking in a microwave oven. Round and ring-shaped dishes are often preferred because these shapes allow microwaves to penetrate the food from various angles. When preparing the recipes in this book, use the size cooking container called for whenever possible. Evenness of cooking and cooking times are often based on amount of food in a particular utensil—just as in conventional cooking.

Caution: Metal utensils are not suitable for microwave cooking. Metal reflects microwaves and, therefore, prevents even cooking. Also, metal utensils can produce arcing, or sparks, within the oven cavity; this can occur when pieces of metal are close to each other. (Remember, the oven walls are made of metal.) Do not use metal pots or pans, thermometers, skewers, colanders, utensils that have metal handles or trim or even metal twist ties. Some oven manufacturers permit the use of *small* pieces of aluminum foil for shielding if pressed firmly against the food or container. Check your owner's manual and follow its directions for use of foil.

MICROWAVED FOODS: IS THERE A DIFFERENCE?

Yes—and no. Some microwaved foods look and taste the same as conventionally cooked foods; some microwaved foods look and/or taste different. Vegetables, for example, can be more visually appealing and flavorful when microwaved because they cook faster and with less moisture. Microwaved cakes achieve more volume and are especially tender. Microwaved muffins and quick breads are also very tender.

On the other hand, the most noticeable difference that some may not consider a plus for microwaving is that many microwaved foods do not brown or attain a crisp crust. Meats and poultry that do not brown are usually less-fatty cuts and smaller pieces that cook quickly. Cakes, breads and other baked items will not develop a firm or browned crust. To compensate for these situations, if desired, several techniques can be used (and are included in the recipes in this book): sauces, glazes, toppings and coatings can be used. Cakes and cupcakes can be frosted. Sauces and glazes contain such ingredients as soy, steak or Worcestershire sauce, soup or gravy mix, bouillon or browning and seasoning sauce. Toppings and coatings contain crumbs, flakes and nuts.

Appetizers

Saucy Cocktail Franks

1 pound (450 g) frankfurters
1½ cups (375 mL) bottled
  barbecue sauce
2 tablespoons (30 mL)
  packed brown sugar
1 teaspoon (5 mL) drained
  prepared horseradish
½ teaspoon (2 mL) dry
  mustard
Tortilla or corn chips, if
  desired

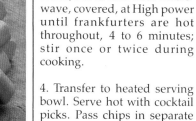

1. Cut frankfurters crosswise into ¾-inch (2 cm) pieces.

2. Place barbecue sauce in 1½-quart (1.5 L) casserole; stir in sugar, horseradish and mustard. Microwave, covered with lid, at High power until sauce is hot, 1½ to 2½ minutes.

3. Add frankfurter pieces to sauce; stir to mix well. Microwave, covered, at High power until frankfurters are hot throughout, 4 to 6 minutes; stir once or twice during cooking.

4. Transfer to heated serving bowl. Serve hot with cocktail picks. Pass chips in separate bowl.

Makes 12 to 16 servings

Spinach Party Dip

1 round loaf (1 pound or
    450 g) crusty bread
2 packages (10 ounces or
    285 g each) frozen
    chopped spinach
2 packages (8 ounces or
    225 g each) cream cheese
¼ cup (60 mL) finely
    chopped green onion
3 tablespoons (45 mL) milk
1 teaspoon (5 mL) lemon
    juice
½ teaspoon (2 mL) dried
    basil, crumbled
½ teaspoon (2 mL) salt
1 small clove garlic, minced
⅛ teaspoon (0.5 mL) pepper
Pinch ground nutmeg

1. Cut 1½-inch (4 cm) thick slice off top of bread. With thin-bladed knife, cut out center of bread; leave sides of bread shell 1 inch (2.5 cm) thick and bottom 2 inches (5 cm) thick. Cut center pieces and top slice into about 1-inch (2.5 cm) cubes; reserve.

2. Microwave spinach in packages at High power until soft, 4½ to 6½ minutes; turn packages over after about half the time. Drain spinach in sieve, pressing with back of spoon to extract as much moisture as possible. Discard liquid.

3. Microwave cream cheese in medium bowl, uncovered, at High power until softened, 30 to 45 seconds. Stir in spinach and remaining ingredients, except bread cubes.

4. Spoon spinach mixture into bread shell; place on plate lined with paper toweling. Microwave, uncovered, at High power until bread is warm, 45 seconds to 1¼ minutes. Serve with reserved bread cubes for dipping. (When bread cubes are used up, cut the bread shell itself into additional cubes, starting at the top.)

Makes 8 to 10 servings

Cheesy Chicken Drumettes

10 chicken drumettes or
    whole wings
¼ cup (60 mL) butter or
    margarine
¼ teaspoon (1 mL) minced
    garlic
½ cup (125 mL) corn flake
    crumbs
¼ cup (60 mL) grated
    Parmesan cheese
½ teaspoon (2 mL) dried
    oregano, crumbled
½ teaspoon (2 mL) dried
    basil, crumbled
½ teaspoon (2 mL) salt
½ teaspoon (2 mL) dry
    mustard
Pinch pepper

1. If using whole chicken wings, cut through each wing at first joint to separate meaty section (drumette) from thin section and wing tip. (Reserve thin sections and tips for making stock or other use.)

2. Starting at narrow end of each drumette and continuing to about ½ inch (1.5 cm) from large end, scrape meat away from bone with knife. Pull meat and skin up and over large end of bone to form a ball.

3. Microwave butter in custard cup, uncovered, at High power until melted, 45 to 60 seconds. Stir in garlic.

4. Place remaining ingredients in small bowl; stir to mix well.

5. Dip meaty end of 1 drumette into butter; shake off excess. Dip into crumb mixture to coat evenly; press crumbs to adhere. Place drumette on roasting rack in baking dish with meaty end toward outside of dish. Repeat until all drumettes have been coated.

6. Microwave, covered with waxed paper, at High power until meat is no longer pink and juices run clear, 4 to 7 minutes; turn drumettes over after half of cooking time.

Makes 4 to 5 servings

Nippy Cheese Dip

1 package (1 pound or
  450 g) processed cheese
  spread
¼ cup (60 mL) beer
1 clove garlic, minced
⅛ teaspoon (0.5 mL) red
  pepper sauce
1 tablespoon (15 mL)
  chopped pimiento
1 tablespoon (15 mL)
  chopped fresh parsley
Tortilla or corn chips

1. Cut cheese spread into
1½-inch (4 cm) cubes; place in
2-quart (2 L) casserole.
Microwave, uncovered, at
Medium (50%) power until
cheese is melted, 3 to 6
minutes; stir once or twice
during cooking.

2. Gradually add beer to
cheese while whisking; whisk
until mixture is smooth. Stir
in garlic and pepper sauce.
Microwave, uncovered, at
High power just until heated
through, about 1 minute.

3. Transfer dip to heated serving bowl. Sprinkle with pimiento and parsley. Serve hot
with chips.

Makes about 2 cups (500 mL)

Canapes Florentine

2 packages (10 ounces or
  285 g each) frozen
  chopped spinach
½ cup (125 mL) finely
  chopped onion
1 tablespoon (15 mL) olive
  oil
1 large clove garlic, minced
2 tablespoons (30 mL)
  all-purpose flour
3 tablespoons (45 mL)
  grated Parmesan cheese
⅛ teaspoon (0.5 mL) ground
  nutmeg
1 package (8 ounces or
  225 g) cream cheese
2 large eggs
6 ounces (170 g) cooked
  ham, minced
¾ cup (180 mL) shredded
  Cheddar cheese
⅛ teaspoon (0.5 mL) dry
  mustard
⅛ teaspoon (0.5 mL) white
  pepper

1. Microwave spinach in
packages at High power until
soft, 4½ to 6½ minutes; turn
packages over after about half
the time. Place spinach in

strainer; press out as much
moisture as possible. Discard
liquid.

2. Combine onion, oil and
garlic in medium bowl.
Microwave, uncovered, at
High power until onion is
tender, 1 to 2 minutes. Add
spinach and flour; stir to mix
well. Stir in Parmesan cheese
and nutmeg.

3. Place 1 tablespoonful
(15 mL) spinach mixture in a
1¾×1¼-inch (4.5×3 cm)
paper nut cup. Spread and
press mixture in even layer on

bottom and sides of nut cup.
Repeat until all spinach mixture is used.

4. Microwave cream cheese in
medium bowl, uncovered, at
Medium (50%) power until
softened, 45 to 60 seconds.
Add remaining ingredients;
stir to mix well.

5. Spoon cream cheese mixture into nut cups, filling just
to top of spinach. Freeze in
single layer on tray until firm.
(If desired, wrap canapes
tightly and freeze up to 1
month.)

6. To cook and serve: Remove
10 to 12 canapes from paper
nut cups. Arrange evenly
spaced on large plate. Microwave, covered with waxed
paper, at Medium (50%)
power just until centers are
set, 8 to 11 minutes; rearrange
canapes on plate every 3
minutes during cooking. Let
stand, covered, 5 to 10
minutes before serving. Repeat with remaining canapes.

Makes about 24 canapes

Soups

Fresh Asparagus Soup

½ cup (125 mL) finely
chopped celery
½ cup (125 mL) finely
chopped onion
2 tablespoons (30 mL) butter
or margarine
1 pound (450 g) fresh
asparagus, chopped
2 teaspoons (10 mL)
chopped fresh parsley
2 teaspoons (10 mL)
chopped fresh basil or
½ teaspoon (2 mL) dried
basil
1⅓ cups (330 mL) chicken
broth
1 cup (250 mL) light cream
or half-and-half
½ teaspoon (2 mL) salt
⅛ teaspoon (0.5 mL) ground
nutmeg
Pinch cayenne pepper
Fresh basil sprigs, if desired

3. Puree asparagus mixture in food processor or blender with on/off turns just until smooth. Return asparagus mixture to casserole.

4. Add broth, cream, salt, nutmeg and pepper to casserole; stir to mix well. Microwave, uncovered, at Medium (50%) power just until hot (do not allow to boil), 7 to 11 minutes; stir soup every 3 minutes during cooking. Garnish with fresh basil sprigs.

Makes 4 servings

1. Combine celery, onion and butter in 2-quart (2 L) casserole. Microwave, covered with lid, at High power until celery and onion are tender, 5 to 7 minutes; stir once after about half of cooking time.

2. Add asparagus to casserole; mix well. Microwave, covered with lid, at High power until asparagus is tender, 4 to 7 minutes; stir once after about half of cooking time. Stir in parsley and chopped basil. Cool mixture slightly.

Quick French Onion Soup

1½ pounds (675 g) yellow onions (about 4 large)
¼ cup (60 mL) butter or margarine
1 can (10¾ ounces or 305 g) condensed chicken broth
1 can (10¾ ounces or 305 g) condensed beef broth
1½ cups (375 mL) water
⅛ teaspoon (0.5 mL) pepper
4 to 8 slices French bread, ¾ inch (2 cm) thick, toasted
1½ cups (375 mL) shredded Swiss cheese (about 6 ounces or 170 g)
⅓ cup (80 mL) grated Parmesan cheese

1. Cut onions crosswise into ¼-inch (0.5 cm) thick slices; place in 3-quart (3 L) casserole. Cut butter into 4 pieces; add to casserole. Microwave, covered with lid, at High power until onions are soft and translucent, 6½ to 8½ minutes; stir once during cooking.

2. Stir onions to separate into rings. Add chicken broth, beef broth, water and pepper; mix well. Microwave, covered, at High power until hot throughout, 4 to 6 minutes.

3. Ladle soup into 4 individual casseroles or bowls, about 2-cup (500 mL) size, dividing evenly. Top with toasted bread slices. Sprinkle with cheeses, dividing evenly. Microwave, uncovered, at High power until cheese is melted, 5 to 7 minutes; rearrange casseroles once or twice during cooking.

Makes 4 servings

Creamy Clam Chowder

4 slices bacon
3 cups (750 mL) pared diced potatoes (⅜-inch or 1 cm cubes)
½ cup (125 mL) chopped onion
2 cans (6½ ounces or 185 g each) minced clams
2 cups (500 mL) milk
1 teaspoon (5 mL) salt
⅛ teaspoon (0.5 mL) pepper
¼ cup (60 mL) all-purpose flour
⅔ cup (160 mL) light cream or half-and-half

1. Cut bacon crosswise into 1-inch (2.5 cm) pieces; spread in bottom of 3-quart (3 L) casserole. Microwave, covered with lid, at High power 3 minutes. Reserve bacon and 2 tablespoons (30 mL) drippings in casserole.

2. Add potatoes and onion to casserole. Drain liquid from clams; add liquid to casserole. Stir to mix. Microwave, covered with lid, at High power

until potatoes are just tender, 7 to 9 minutes; stir once during cooking.

3. Add 1⅔ cups (410 mL) of the milk, the salt and pepper

to casserole. Mix flour and remaining ⅓ cup (80 mL) milk in a cup until smooth. Add flour mixture to casserole; stir to mix well. Microwave, uncovered, at High power until thickened, 8 to 10 minutes; stir every 2 minutes.

4. Add clams and light cream to casserole; stir to mix well. Microwave, uncovered, at High power just until chowder is hot, 2 to 4 minutes; do not boil.

Makes 4 servings

Holiday Turkey

¼ cup (60 mL) butter or margarine, if desired
1 teaspoon (5 mL) browning sauce, if desired
12-pound (5.5 kg) ready-to-cook turkey, giblets removed*

Turkey should fit comfortably in microwave oven; there should be a minimum of 3 inches (8 cm) space between turkey and oven walls and 2 inches (5 cm) space between turkey and top of oven cavity.

1. Microwave butter in custard cup, uncovered, at High power until melted, 30 to 45 seconds. Stir in browning sauce; reserve.

2. Place turkey breast-side-down in large baking dish. Microwave, uncovered, at High power 10 minutes. Then microwave at Medium (50%) power 27 minutes; if some areas of turkey are browning too quickly, shield these areas with small individual pieces of aluminum foil.

3. Turn turkey on its side. Microwave at Medium (50%) power 37 minutes; baste turkey with butter mixture and shield with foil as needed.

4. Turn turkey on its other side. Microwave at Medium (50%) power 37 minutes; baste and shield with foil as needed.

5. Turn turkey breast-side-up. Microwave at Medium (50%) power until legs move freely and juices run clear when pierced deep between leg and thigh, 40 to 50 minutes; baste and shield with foil as needed. When removed from oven, internal temperature should register 170°F to 175°F (77°C to 79°C) when tested for 1 minute with meat thermometer in thickest part of thigh.

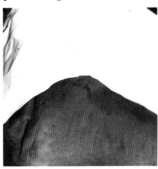

6. Let stand, tented with foil, at least 20 minutes and up to 45 minutes before carving. Internal temperature should register 185°F (85°C) after standing 10 to 15 minutes. Serve turkey with Easy Cornbread Dressing (recipe follows).

Makes about 12 servings

Easy Cornbread Dressing

8 slices bacon, cut into ½-inch (1.5 cm) pieces
2 cups (500 mL) chopped celery
1 cup (250 mL) chopped onion
½ cup (125 mL) butter
2 cans (10¾ ounces or 305 g each) chicken broth
½ to ¾ cup (125 to 180 mL) hot water, if desired
2 tablespoons (30 mL) chopped fresh parsley
1½ teaspoons (7 mL) poultry seasoning
1 package (16 ounces or 450 g) cornbread stuffing mix
3 cups (750 mL) croutons

1. Place bacon in 5-quart (5 L) casserole. Microwave, covered with paper toweling, at High power until bacon is crisp, 6 to 7 minutes; stir twice during cooking. Drain bacon on paper toweling; remove drippings from casserole.

2. Add celery, onion and butter to casserole. Microwave, uncovered, at High power until vegetables are tender, 6 to 8 minutes; stir twice during cooking. Stir in bacon, broth, water (if moister dressing is desired), parsley, and poultry seasoning. Add stuffing mix and croutons; stir until well mixed and evenly moistened.

3. Microwave dressing, uncovered, at High power until hot throughout, 7 to 10 minutes; toss and stir twice during cooking. (Dressing can stand, covered, up to 35 minutes before serving.)

Makes about 12 servings

Cranberry-Glazed Chicken

1 can (16 ounces or 450 g)
    whole cranberry sauce
1 tablespoon (15 mL)
    packed brown sugar
1 tablespoon (15 mL) frozen
    orange juice concentrate,
    thawed
1 teaspoon (5 mL) Dijon-
    style mustard
¼ teaspoon (1 mL) salt
1 tablespoon (15 mL) water
1 teaspoon (5 mL) browning
    sauce
1 broiler-fryer chicken,
    quartered (about
    3 pounds or 1350 g)
1 seedless orange, if desired
Fresh parsley sprigs, if
    desired

1. Combine cranberry sauce, sugar, orange juice concentrate, mustard and salt in medium bowl; stir to mix well. Reserve glaze.

2. Mix water and browning sauce in a cup. Remove skin from chicken, if desired. Arrange chicken pieces, evenly spaced and bony side up, on roasting rack. Brush chicken

pieces with ½ the browning sauce mixture. Microwave, covered with waxed paper, at High power 10 minutes. (Drain drippings from rack.) Brush chicken lightly with cranberry glaze.

3. Turn chicken pieces over; brush with remaining browning sauce mixture. Microwave, covered with waxed paper, at High power 5 minutes.

4. Brush chicken pieces with cranberry glaze. Microwave, covered with waxed paper, at High power until chicken is no longer pink inside, 4 to 7 minutes. Transfer chicken to serving dish.

5. Microwave remaining cranberry glaze, covered with waxed paper, at High power just until hot, about 1 minute. Slice orange; cut slices in half. Garnish chicken with orange slices and parsley; serve with remaining glaze.

Makes 4 servings

Jade Chicken Stir-Fry

1 pound (450 g) skinless,
    boneless chicken breasts
3 tablespoons (45 mL) soy
    sauce
2 tablespoons (30 mL) rice
    wine or dry sherry
1 teaspoon (5 mL) sugar
1 teaspoon (5 mL) minced
    pared fresh ginger root
1 small clove garlic, minced
1 tablespoon (15 mL)
    cornstarch
1 package (6 ounces or
    170 g) frozen snow peas
2 tablespoons (30 mL)
    peanut or vegetable oil
1 cup (250 mL) thinly sliced
    celery
8 ounces (225 g) fresh
    spinach, torn into bite-
    size pieces
⅓ cup (80 mL) slivered
    blanched almonds

1. Cut chicken crosswise into ½-inch (1.5 cm) wide strips; place in medium bowl. Stir in soy sauce, rice wine, sugar, ginger and garlic. Sprinkle with cornstarch; mix well. Marinate at room temperature 20 to 30 minutes.

2. Microwave snow peas in package at High power until soft, 1½ to 2½ minutes. Drain well.

3. Preheat 10-inch (25 cm) browning dish according to manufacturer's directions. Add oil to dish; swirl to coat.

4. Add chicken and marinade to browning dish; stir immediately to prevent sticking. Microwave, uncovered, at High power 2 minutes; stir after 1 minute of cooking.

5. Stir celery into chicken mixture. Microwave, covered with lid, at High power 1 minute. Stir in spinach and snow peas. Microwave, covered, just until vegetables are crisp-tender, 2 to 4 minutes; stir after about half of cooking time.

6. Sprinkle almonds over chicken mixture; stir to mix well. Serve immediately.

Makes 3 to 4 servings

Deep-Dish Turkey Pie

1 package (10 ounces or 285 g) frozen cut asparagus
¼ cup (60 mL) plus 3 to 3½ tablespoons (45 to 52 mL) water
¼ cup (60 mL) all-purpose flour
1 teaspoon (5 mL) powdered American cheese food
½ teaspoon (2 mL) salt
1½ tablespoons (22 mL) solid vegetable shortening
Paprika
2 tablespoons (30 mL) cornstarch
1 teaspoon (5 mL) chicken bouillon granules
¼ teaspoon (1 mL) dried thyme
⅛ teaspoon (0.5 mL) ground sage
Pinch pepper
½ cup (125 mL) milk
¼ cup (60 mL) chopped onion
1½ cups (375 mL) diced cooked turkey
⅔ cup (160 mL) shredded pared carrot

1. Place asparagus and 2 tablespoons (30 mL) water in 1-quart (1 L) casserole. Microwave, covered with lid, at High power until asparagus is soft, 3 to 5 minutes; stir after about half the time to break pieces apart. Drain asparagus; reserve, covered.

2. Combine flour, cheese food and ¼ teaspoon (1 mL) salt in medium bowl. Cut in shortening until mixture resembles small peas. Sprinkle 1 tablespoon (15 mL) of the water over flour mixture while stirring with fork.* Using ½ tablespoon (7 mL) water, add only as much as needed for dough to form ball.

3. Roll out dough on floured surface into 6-inch (15 cm) circle; cut into quarters. Pierce pastry all over with fork; place on sheet of waxed paper. Sprinkle pastry with paprika. Microwave, uncovered, at High power until dry and flaky, 1 to 2 minutes. Cool on wire rack.

4. For sauce, mix cornstarch, bouillon, thyme, sage, pepper and remaining ¼ teaspoon (1 mL) salt in medium bowl. Add the remaining ¼ cup (60 mL) water; stir until cornstarch dissolves. Stir in milk and onion.

5. Microwave sauce, uncovered, at High power until onion is tender and sauce is thickened, 2½ to 4 minutes; stir every minute during cooking.

6. Add turkey, carrot and sauce to asparagus in casserole; stir to mix well. Microwave, uncovered, at High power until hot and bubbly, 3 to 5 minutes; stir every 2 minutes during cooking. Top casserole with pastry. Microwave, uncovered, 1 minute to heat pastry.

Makes 4 servings

If yellower pastry is desired, add 1 or 2 drops yellow food coloring to water before sprinkling over flour.

Chicken Ranchero

¾ cup (180 mL) tomato sauce
1 small onion, finely chopped
2 tablespoons (30 mL) finely chopped celery
2 tablespoons (30 mL) packed brown sugar
2 tablespoons (30 mL) cider vinegar
1 tablespoon (15 mL) light corn syrup
1 tablespoon (15 mL) Worcestershire sauce
¾ teaspoon (4 mL) dry mustard
1 small clove garlic, minced
½ teaspoon (2 mL) salt
¼ teaspoon (1 mL) paprika
¼ teaspoon (1 mL) ground cumin
1 broiler-fryer chicken (3 pounds or 1350 g), cut into 8 pieces
Fresh parsley sprigs, if desired

1. For barbecue sauce, combine all ingredients, except chicken and parsley, in 4-cup (1 L) measure; mix well. Microwave, covered with waxed paper, at High power until hot, about 3 minutes; stir once during cooking. Microwave, covered, at Medium (50%) power until onion is tender and flavors are blended, 12 to 15 minutes; stir every 3 minutes during cooking.

2. Arrange chicken pieces in 13×9-inch (33×23 cm) baking dish in single layer with meatiest portions toward outside.

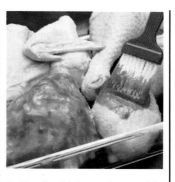

3. Brush chicken pieces with barbecue sauce. Microwave chicken, covered with waxed paper, at High power for 9 minutes; rotate dish ½ turn after half of cooking time.

4. Rearrange chicken pieces in dish so that less-cooked portions are toward outside. Brush chicken with sauce.

5. Microwave, covered with waxed paper, at High power until chicken is cooked through (no longer pink near the bone) and tender, 8 to 14 minutes; rotate dish ½ turn after about half of cooking time. Brush chicken lightly with any remaining sauce. Transfer to serving plate. Garnish with parsley.

Makes 4 to 6 servings

Stuffed Cornish Hens Orangerie

STUFFING
½ cup (125 mL) hot water
½ cup (125 mL) uncooked
  instant rice
2 tablespoons (30 mL) butter
1 large orange
⅔ cup (160 mL) lightly
  packed, chopped lettuce
2 tablespoons (30 mL)
  minced onion
2 tablespoons (30 mL)
  chopped walnuts
¼ teaspoon (1 mL) ground
  ginger
¼ teaspoon (1 mL) salt
Pinch ground allspice

2 Cornish game hens (1½
  pounds or 675 g each)

GLAZE
½ cup (125 mL) orange juice
1 tablespoon (15 mL)
  cornstarch
2 tablespoons (30 mL) dry
  sherry
1 tablespoon (15 mL) soy
  sauce
1 tablespoon (15 mL)
  packed brown sugar
Pinch ground allspice

1. For Stuffing: Microwave water in 4-cup (1 L) measure, covered with plastic wrap, at High power until boiling, 1 to 1½ minutes. Stir in rice; reserve, covered. Microwave butter in custard cup, uncovered, at High power until melted, 30 to 45 seconds.

2. Grate ¼ teaspoon (1 mL) rind from orange. Peel orange; remove seeds and white membranes. Chop orange segments coarsely.

3. Add chopped orange, the butter, lettuce, onion, walnuts, ginger, salt, orange rind

and allspice to rice; stir to mix well. Spoon rice stuffing into body cavities of hens, dividing evenly; secure opening with wooden picks. Place hens, breast-side-down, on roasting rack.

4. For Glaze: Measure orange juice into 1-cup (250 mL) measure. Stir in cornstarch until dissolved. Stir in sherry, soy sauce, brown sugar and allspice. Microwave, uncovered, at High power until glaze is thickened, 1½ to 2 minutes; stir 2 or 3 times during cooking. Brush hens with ½ of the glaze.

5. Cover hens with waxed paper. Microwave at High power 8 minutes; rotate rack ½ turn every 2 or 3 minutes during cooking.

6. Turn hens breast-side-up; brush with remaining glaze. Microwave, covered with waxed paper, at High power until juices run clear and meat near bone is no longer pink, 8 to 12 minutes; rotate rack ½ turn every 2 or 3 minutes. Let hens stand, covered, 5 minutes before serving.

Makes 2 servings

Oven-Fried Chicken

½ cup (125 mL) instant
  mashed potato flakes
½ cup (125 mL) seasoned
  fine dry bread crumbs
1 teaspoon (5 mL) dried
  parsley flakes
¼ teaspoon (1 mL) salt
Pinch pepper
⅓ cup (80 mL) butter or
  margarine
¼ teaspoon (1 mL) prepared
  mustard
2½ pounds (1125 g) cut up
  broiler-fryer chicken
  pieces

1. Combine potato flakes, bread crumbs, parsley, salt and pepper in shallow dish or pie plate. Stir to mix well.

2. Microwave butter in second shallow dish, uncovered, at High power until melted, 45 to 60 seconds. Stir in mustard.

3. Pat chicken dry with paper toweling. Dip chicken pieces into butter mixture to coat all sides; shake off excess. Roll in bread crumb mixture to coat evenly; press coating gently but firmly against chicken.

4. Arrange chicken pieces on roasting rack, bone-side-down, with meatiest portions toward outside of rack. Microwave chicken, uncovered, at High power 9 minutes. Rearrange chicken pieces so that less-cooked portions are toward outside of rack; do not turn pieces over.

5. Microwave, uncovered, at High power until juices run clear and chicken is no longer pink near the bone, 8 to 12 minutes.

Makes 4 to 5 servings

Regal Crown Roast of Pork

STUFFING
- 1½ pounds (675 g) ground pork
- ½ cup (125 mL) thinly sliced celery
- ½ cup (125 mL) chopped onion
- ¼ cup (60 mL) butter or margarine
- ⅓ cup (80 mL) chopped spiced peaches
- 2 cups (500 mL) fresh white bread cubes
- 2 cups (500 mL) fresh rye bread cubes
- ¼ cup (60 mL) raisins
- 3 tablespoons (45 mL) chopped fresh parsley
- ¾ teaspoon (4 mL) poultry seasoning
- ½ teaspoon (2 mL) salt
- ⅛ teaspoon (0.5 mL) pepper

ROAST
- 6½ pounds (3 kg) pork crown rib roast
- 1 teaspoon (5 mL) dried marjoram leaves, crushed
- 1 teaspoon (5 mL) seasoned salt
- ½ teaspoon (2 mL) poultry seasoning
- Whole spiced peaches, if desired
- Coriander, if desired

1. For Stuffing: Microwave ground pork, uncovered, in 3-quart (3 L) casserole at High power until meat is no longer pink, 5 to 9 minutes; stir twice during cooking. Drain well; reserve.

2. Combine celery, onion and butter in 1-quart (1 L) casserole. Microwave, uncovered, at High power until celery is tender, 3 to 5 minutes.

3. Add celery mixture and remaining stuffing ingredients to ground pork; mix well. Cover and reserve.

4. For Roast: Place roast bone-end-down on roasting rack. Mix marjoram, seasoned salt and poultry seasoning in small bowl; rub mixture onto roast. Microwave, uncovered, at High power 5 minutes. Then microwave at Medium (50%) power 45 to 50 minutes; rotate ½ turn after about half of cooking time.

5. Turn roast over. Fill cavity lightly with stuffing; cover stuffing with plastic wrap. [Place any leftover stuffing in 1½-quart (1.5 L) casserole; cover and refrigerate.]

6. Microwave roast at Medium (50%) power 50 to 55 minutes; rotate ½ turn after about half of cooking time. Remove roast from oven. Test for doneness: internal temperature of meat must be at least 165°F (74°C) when tested with meat thermometer in several places. If temperature is below 165°F (74°C), microwave roast additional 10 to 12 minutes and test again. [Temperature of meat will rise to 170°F (77°C) during standing time.]

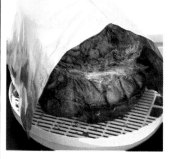

7. Tent roast loosely with aluminum foil. Let stand 10 minutes. (Meanwhile, microwave leftover stuffing in casserole, covered, at High power until hot, 4 to 5 minutes; stir once during cooking.)

8. Transfer roast to serving platter. Place paper frills on bone ends; garnish with whole spiced peaches and coriander. Carve roast between bones. Serve with stuffing.

Makes 8 to 12 servings

Hungarian Veal Dinner

4 veal cutlets (about 1
  pound or 450 g)
2 cups (500 mL) all-purpose
  flour
¾ teaspoon (4 mL) salt
½ teaspoon (2 mL) paprika
½ teaspoon (2 mL) dried
  tarragon leaves, crushed
⅛ teaspoon (0.5 mL) pepper
4 tablespoons (60 mL) butter
  or margarine
2 medium onions, cut into
  quarters
2 teaspoons (10 mL) baking
  powder
2 teaspoons (10 mL) poppy
  seeds
1 teaspoon (5 mL) dried
  chives
¼ cup (60 mL) milk
1 large egg
⅓ cup (80 mL) seasoned dry
  bread crumbs
1 can (10¾ ounces or 305 g)
  condensed cream of
  chicken soup
1 can (4 ounces or 115 g)
  sliced mushrooms,
  undrained

1. Lightly pound each cutlet with meat mallet to ¼-inch (0.5 cm) thickness. Place 1 cup (250 mL) of the flour, ½ teaspoon (2 mL) of the salt, the paprika, tarragon and pepper into plastic bag; shake bag to mix. Add cutlets to bag, 1 at a time; shake to coat well.

2. Place butter in 12×8-inch (30×20 cm) baking dish. Microwave, uncovered, at High power until butter is melted and very hot, about 2 minutes. Remove 2 tablespoons (30 mL) butter to 1-cup (250 mL) measure; reserve.

3. Add cutlets and onions to baking dish. Microwave, covered with plastic wrap, at High power 2 minutes. Then microwave at Medium (50%) power until veal is tender, 9 to 11 minutes; rotate dish ½ turn after about half of cooking time.

4. Meanwhile, combine remaining 1 cup (250 mL) flour and ¼ teaspoon (1 mL) salt, the baking powder, poppy seeds and chives in small bowl. Add milk and egg to reserved butter; mix well. Stir milk mixture into flour mixture to form slightly stiff dough. Place bread crumbs in second small bowl. Drop dough by heaping tablespoonful into crumbs; roll to coat. Reserve dumplings.

5. Remove veal from oven. Combine soup and mushrooms in small bowl. Microwave, uncovered, at High power until heated, about 3 minutes; stir once during cooking.

6. Pour soup mixture over veal. Top with dumplings. Microwave, covered with plastic wrap, at High power until dumplings are firm, 5 to 6 minutes; rotate ½ turn after 3 minutes of cooking. Let stand 5 minutes.

Makes 4 servings

Homestyle Pot Roast

3 to 3½ pounds (1350 to
  1600 g) boneless beef
  chuck roast
1 can (8 ounces or 225 g)
  tomato sauce
½ tablespoon (7 mL) instant
  beef bouillon granules
½ teaspoon (2 mL) dried
  ground marjoram
½ teaspoon (2 mL) salt
1 bay leaf
4 medium carrots
1 medium onion
1 large potato, pared

1. Cut 1-inch (2.5 cm) strip from open end of large plastic cooking bag to use as closure. Place roast in cooking bag; set bag in 12×8-inch (30×20 cm) baking dish.

2. Mix together tomato sauce, bouillon granules, marjoram and salt in 2-cup (500 mL) measure; pour over roast in bag. Add bay leaf to bag. Gather end of bag; tie loosely with plastic strip, leaving small space for steam to escape.

3. Microwave at High power 10 minutes, rotating dish ½ turn after 5 minutes. Microwave at Medium (50%) power 25 minutes.

4. Meanwhile, cut carrots crosswise into 1-inch (25 cm) lengths; cut any thick pieces in half lengthwise. Cut onion into 8 even wedges. Cut potato into ½-inch (1.5 cm) cubes.

5. Turn roast and bag over. Open cooking bag carefully— escaping steam can burn.

Add carrots, onion and potato to bag and retie loosely.

6. Microwave at Medium (50%) power until roast and vegetables are tender, 30 to 40 minutes. Let stand in closed bag 10 minutes. Remove roast and vegetables to serving platter; discard bay leaf. Top with sauce.

Makes 6 to 8 servings

Meatballs Oriental

2 cans (8 ounces or 225 g each) pineapple chunks in natural juice
¼ cup (60 mL) cornstarch
1 cup (250 mL) chicken broth
½ cup (125 mL) packed brown sugar
½ cup (125 mL) cider vinegar
2 tablespoons (30 mL) rice wine or dry sherry
5 tablespoons (75 mL) soy sauce
½ pound (225 g) ground beef
½ pound (225 g) lean ground pork
1 large egg, lightly beaten
¼ cup (60 mL) fine dry bread crumbs
2 tablespoons (30 mL) minced green onion
1 teaspoon (5 mL) minced fresh ginger root
⅛ teaspoon (0.5 mL) black pepper
1 large green bell pepper, cut into thin strips
3 cups (750 mL) hot cooked rice

1. Drain pineapple, reserving ½ cup (125 mL) of the juice. Mix cornstarch and the reserved juice in 2-quart (2 L) casserole until smooth. Stir in broth, sugar, vinegar, rice wine and 3 tablespoons (45 mL) of the soy sauce; stir until sugar dissolves.

2. Microwave sauce mixture, uncovered, at High power until thick and shiny, 7 to 9 minutes; stir with whisk twice during cooking. Reserve sauce.

3. While sauce is cooking, combine beef, pork, egg, bread crumbs, onion, ginger, black pepper and remaining 2 tablespoons (30 mL) soy sauce in medium bowl; mix well. Shape into 20 meatballs, 1 to 1½ inches (2.5 to 4 cm) in diameter. Place balls in 12×8-inch (30×20 cm) baking dish.

4. Scatter green pepper over meatballs. Microwave, uncovered, at High power until meatballs are cooked through and no longer pink inside, 6 to 8 minutes; stir mixture to rearrange once during cooking.

5. Drain fat from meatballs. Add meatballs, green pepper and pineapple to reserved sauce; stir to mix well. Microwave, uncovered, at High power until hot, 4 to 6 minutes; stir once during heating. Serve over hot cooked rice.

Makes 4 servings

Ham & Broccoli Divan

2 packages (8 ounces or 225 g each) frozen broccoli spears
1 can (10¾ ounces or 305 g) condensed cream of mushroom soup
¼ cup (60 mL) milk
1 teaspoon (5 mL) prepared mustard
½ teaspoon (2 mL) Worcestershire sauce
Pinch pepper
2 cups (500 mL) diced cooked ham (about ½-inch or 1.5 cm cubes)*
1 can (3 ounces or 85 g) French-fried onion rings
1 cup (250 mL) shredded Cheddar cheese

Diced cooked chicken can be substituted for the ham, if desired.

1. Microwave broccoli in packages at High power just until soft, 6 to 8 minutes; turn packages over after about half of time. Drain well.

2. Mix soup, milk, mustard, Worcestershire sauce and pepper in 4-cup (1 L) measure until smooth. Microwave, covered with waxed paper, at High power until hot, 3 to 4 minutes; stir twice during cooking.

3. Arrange broccoli spears crosswise in 12×8-inch (30×20 cm) baking dish, alternating heads and stems from one side of dish to the other. Arrange ham in even layer down center of dish, leaving broccoli heads uncovered. Top ham with half the onion rings in even layer. Sprinkle cheese evenly over onion rings. Pour soup mixture evenly over cheese.

4. Microwave casserole, covered with waxed paper, at High power just until broccoli is crisp-tender, 5 to 7 minutes; rotate dish ½ turn after about half of cooking time.

5. Sprinkle remaining onion rings evenly over top of casserole. Microwave, uncovered, at High power until hot throughout, 4 to 6 minutes; rotate dish ½ turn after about half of cooking time.

Makes 4 to 6 servings

Classic Lemon Lamb Chops

4 loin lamb chops (1 inch or
  2.5 cm thick)
¼ cup (60 mL) lemon juice
¼ cup (60 mL) olive oil
¼ cup (60 mL) chopped
  onion
1 small clove garlic, minced
¼ teaspoon (1 mL) dried
  thyme
¼ teaspoon (1 mL) dried
  rosemary, crumbled
¼ teaspoon (1 mL) salt
1 bay leaf
Pinch pepper
4 pieces leaf lettuce, if
  desired
Lemon slices, if desired

1. Place lamb chops in shallow glass dish. Whisk lemon juice and oil in small bowl until blended; stir in onion, garlic, thyme, rosemary, salt, bay leaf and pepper. Pour marinade over chops; turn chops to coat all sides. Marinate, covered, at room temperature, turning occasionally, 30 minutes.

2. Remove chops from marinade and blot dry with paper toweling; discard marinade. Preheat 10-inch (25 cm) browning dish according to manufacturer's directions.

3. Place chops, evenly spaced, in browning dish. Microwave, uncovered, at High power 1 minute.

4. Turn chops over. Microwave, uncovered, at High power until meat is lightly springy and resistant to the touch, 1½ to 2½ minutes. Meat will be medium-rare.*

5. Immediately transfer chops to serving platter lined with lettuce leaves. Garnish with lemon slices.

Makes 4 servings

For medium or well-done chops, microwave about 30 seconds longer in Step 3 and 1 to 1½ minutes longer in Step 4. Juices will appear on top and meat will become increasingly firm as it becomes more well-done. Do not overcook.

Flank Steak Roll-Up

1½ pounds (675 g) flank
  steak
1 can (8 ounces or 225 g)
  tomato sauce
1 envelope (1½ ounces or
  45 g) onion soup mix
1 teaspoon (5 mL)
  Worcestershire sauce
1 small clove garlic, minced
1 package (10 ounces or
  285 g) frozen cut green
  beans
1 cup (250 mL) shredded
  pared potato
½ cup (125 mL) chopped
  green onion
Parsley sprigs, if desired

1. Pound flank steak with
meat mallet to tenderize and
to flatten to about ½-inch
(1.5 cm) thick.

2. Mix tomato sauce, soup
mix, Worcestershire sauce
and garlic in 2-cup (500 mL)
measure. Spread ½ the to-
mato marinade in 8×8-inch
(20×20 cm) baking dish. Place
meat in baking dish; spread
with remaining marinade. Refrigerate, covered with plastic
wrap, at least 8 hours or
overnight.

3. Microwave green beans in
package at High power just
until soft, 3 to 4 minutes; turn
package over after about half
of time. Drain well.

4. Scrape tomato marinade off
both sides of meat and from
dish into 2-cup (500 mL) measure. Microwave marinade,
uncovered, at High power
until hot, 1 to 1½ minutes.

5. Combine potato and green
onion in small bowl. Microwave, uncovered, at High
power until hot, 1 to 2 minutes. Stir in beans.

6. Spread flank steak out flat.
Top with potato mixture;
spread in an even layer. Roll
up meat, jelly-roll style. Secure seam with wooden
picks. Place roll, seam-side-

up in 8×8-inch (20×20 cm)
baking dish. Spoon heated
marinade over meat.

7. Microwave meat, covered
with plastic wrap, at High
power 5 minutes. Microwave,
covered, at Medium (50%)
power until meat is fork tender, 20 to 25 minutes; turn
meat seam-side-down and
baste with marinade after
about half of cooking time.
Let meat stand, covered, 5 to
10 minutes before slicing.
Garnish with parsley sprigs.

Makes 4 servings

Hearty German Supper

4 medium potatoes, pared
½ teaspoon (2 mL) salt
¾ cup (180 mL) water
4 slices bacon
½ cup (125 mL) chopped
  onion
¼ cup (60 mL) sugar
2 tablespoons (30 mL) all-
  purpose flour
½ teaspoon (2 mL) dill seed
¼ teaspoon (1 mL) dried
  thyme, crumbled
⅛ teaspoon (0.5 mL) dry
  mustard
Pinch pepper
⅓ cup (80 mL) white wine
  vinegar
¼ cup (60 mL) dry white
  wine
4 smoked bratwurst or
  knockwurst

1. Cut potatoes into ¾-inch (2
cm) cubes; combine with salt
and ¼ cup (60 mL) water in
2-quart (2 L) casserole.
Microwave, covered with lid,
at High power until potatoes
are fork-tender, 9 to 12
minutes; stir once after about
half of cooking time. Drain
potatoes.

2. Arrange bacon in single
layer on roasting rack placed
in 12×8-inch (30×20 cm) baking dish. Microwave, covered
with paper toweling, at High
power until slightly under-

done, 3 to 4 minutes. Let
stand, covered, 5 minutes to
complete cooking.

3. Remove bacon and rack
from baking dish, reserving
all bacon drippings in baking
dish. Stir in onion. Microwave, uncovered, at High
power until onion is tender,
1½ to 2½ minutes. Add sugar, flour, dill seed, thyme,
mustard and pepper; stir until
no lumps of flour remain.

4. Stir vinegar, wine and the
remaining ½ cup (125 mL) water into onion mixture. Micro-

wave, uncovered, at High
power until dressing thickens, 4 to 6 minutes; stir twice
during cooking. Crumble bacon; add to dressing. Gently
stir in potatoes.

5. Pierce each sausage in 2
places with fork to prevent
bursting; arrange on top of
potato salad. Microwave, uncovered, at High power until
sausages are hot, 5½ to 7 minutes; rearrange sausages after
about half of cooking time.

Makes 4 servings

Double-Decker Pork Chops

1 cup (250 mL) chopped unpared apple (about 1 medium)
¼ cup (60 mL) raisins
1 tablespoon (15 mL) butter or margarine
⅛ teaspoon (0.5 mL) ground cinnamon
⅛ teaspoon (0.5 mL) dried thyme
½ cup (125 mL) seasoned dry bread crumbs
2 teaspoons (10 mL) brown sugar
1 package (10 ounces or 285 g) frozen Brussels sprouts
8 pork loin chops, ¼-inch (0.5 cm) thick (about 1½ pounds or 675 g)

1. Combine apple, raisins, butter, cinnamon and thyme in 2-cup (500 mL) measure. Microwave, uncovered, at High power until apple is tender, 2 to 3 minutes. Stir in ¼ cup (60 mL) of the bread crumbs and the brown sugar. Reserve stuffing.

2. Microwave Brussels sprouts in package at High power until slightly warm, about 3 minutes; turn package over after 1½ minutes. Remove sprouts from package and drain; wrap in plastic wrap.

3. Spread ¼ of stuffing (about ¼ cup or 60 mL) on each of 4 pork chops. Top each with another chop; secure with wooden picks.

4. Spread remaining ¼ cup (60 mL) bread crumbs in flat dish. Press pork chops into crumbs to coat both sides. Arrange chops around outer edges of roasting rack in 13×9-inch (33×23 cm) baking dish, with meaty portions toward outside of dish.

5. Microwave, uncovered, at High power 5 minutes. Place wrapped Brussels sprouts in center of roasting rack with pork chops. Microwave, uncovered, at Medium (50%) power until meat is no longer pink, 20 to 24 minutes; rearrange pork chops after about half of cooking time.

Makes 4 servings

Beefy Cabbage Rolls

1 head green cabbage
1½ cups (375 mL) sliced fresh mushrooms
1 can (16 ounces or 450 g) tomatoes, chopped and drained
2 cups (500 mL) shredded cooked beef
1 cup (250 mL) shredded pared carrot
⅔ cup (160 mL) chopped onion
1 teaspoon (5 mL) dried basil
1 clove garlic, minced
½ teaspoon (2 mL) salt
¼ teaspoon (1 mL) dried rosemary
¼ teaspoon (1 mL) grated lemon rind
⅛ teaspoon (0.5 mL) pepper
2 tablespoons (30 mL) olive oil
1 can (15 ounces or 425 g) tomato sauce
2 tablespoons (30 mL) packed brown sugar
1 tablespoon (15 mL) cider vinegar
1 teaspoon (5 mL) instant beef bouillon granules

1. Cut center core from cabbage; discard. Wrap cabbage in plastic wrap; microwave at High power just until outer leaves can be separated from head, 1½ to 3½ minutes.

2. Remove 8 cabbage leaves; cut out hard center rib at base of each leaf. Spread leaves on baking sheet. Microwave, covered with plastic wrap, at High power until pliable, 1 to 2½ minutes. Reserve.

3. Shred enough of the remaining cabbage to make 1½ cups (375 mL). (Refrigerate remaining cabbage, wrapped in plastic, for other use.) Combine shredded cabbage and mushrooms in 2-quart (2 L) casserole. Microwave, covered with lid, at High power until cabbage is tender, 3 to 6 minutes; stir twice during cooking. Drain well.

4. Add tomatoes, beef, carrot, ⅓ cup (80 mL) onion, ½ teaspoon (2 mL) basil, the garlic, salt, rosemary, lemon rind and pepper to mushroom mixture; mix well.

5. Spoon ⅛ of the beef filling onto center of each cabbage leaf. Fold sides of each leaf over filling; roll up securely and fasten at seam with wooden pick. Place rolls, seam-side-down in 12×8-inch (30×20 cm) baking dish.

6. For sauce, combine remaining ⅓ cup (80 mL) onion and the oil in medium bowl. Microwave, uncovered, at High power until onion is tender, 2 to 3 minutes. Stir in the remaining ½ teaspoon (2 mL) basil and the remaining ingredients. Microwave, uncovered, at High power until sauce is thickened, 8 to 12 minutes; stir 2 or 3 times during cooking.

7. Pour sauce over cabbage rolls. Microwave, covered with plastic wrap, at High power until heated through, 6 to 10 minutes; rotate dish ½ turn twice during cooking. Let stand 5 minutes before serving.

Makes 4 servings

Pineapple-Glazed Ham

3 pounds (1350 g) fully
   cooked boneless ham, in
   one piece
1 jar (10 ounces or 285 g)
   pineapple or apricot
   preserves
2 tablespoons (30 mL)
   Dijon-style mustard
Endive, if desired
Spiced crab apples, if
   desired

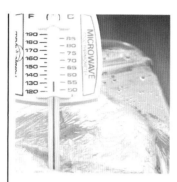

1. Place ham, fat-side-down, in 12×8-inch (30×20 cm) baking dish. Microwave, covered with plastic wrap, at Medium (50%) power 20 minutes.

2. Meanwhile, combine preserves and mustard; stir to mix well.

3. Turn ham over. Score ham ¼-inch (0.5 cm) deep on fat side as follows: Make series of diagonal cuts 1-inch (2.5 cm) apart. Make second set of diagonal cuts 1-inch (2.5 cm) apart in opposite direction to form diamond shapes. Spread evenly with ¾ of the preserves mixture.

4. Cover ham with plastic wrap; insert microwave-safe thermometer through plastic so tip is in center of meat. Microwave at Medium (50%) power until internal temperature reaches 130°F (55°C), 10 to 15 minutes. Remove plastic; spread remaining preserves mixture on ham.

5. Cover ham with loose tent of aluminum foil, shiny side facing inward. Let stand 10 minutes. Transfer ham to serving platter; garnish with endive and crab apples.

Makes 8 to 10 servings

Cannelloni Romana

½ pound (225 g) mild
 Italian sausage
1 small onion, finely
 chopped
1 small clove garlic, minced
1 pound (450 g) ricotta
 cheese, drained
1 cup (250 mL) shredded
 mozzarella cheese
½ cup (125 mL) grated
 Parmesan cheese
2 large eggs
2 tablespoons (30 mL)
 minced fresh parsley
½ teaspoon (2 mL) salt
½ teaspoon (2 mL) dried
 oregano, crumbled
¼ teaspoon (1 mL) dried
 basil, crumbled
Pinch pepper
1 jar (15½ ounces or 440 g)
 spaghetti sauce
½ teaspoon (2 mL) dried
 marjoram, crumbled
8 cooked cannelloni shells

1. Remove sausage from casings; crumble into microwave-safe colander.* Place colander in 2-quart (2 L) casserole. Microwave, un-

covered, at High power until sausage is no longer pink, 2 to 4 minutes; stir with fork to break up meat once during cooking.

2. Discard drippings from casserole. Transfer sausage from colander to casserole; break up into small pieces with back of spoon. Stir in onion and garlic. Microwave, uncovered, at High power until onion is tender, 2 to 3 minutes.

3. Combine ricotta cheese, ½ cup (125 mL) of the mozzarella cheese, ¼ cup (60 mL)

of the Parmesan cheese, the eggs, parsley, salt, oregano, basil and pepper in medium bowl; mix well.

4. Add spaghetti sauce and marjoram to sausage mixture; stir to mix well. Microwave, uncovered, at High power until hot, 1½ to 3 minutes; stir once during cooking. Spread about ⅓ of the meat sauce in 12×8-inch (30×20 cm) baking dish.

5. Spoon cheese mixture into cannelloni shells; arrange in a row in baking dish.

6. Pour the remaining sauce over cannelloni. Microwave, covered with waxed paper, at High power until hot, 11 to 13 minutes; rotate dish ½ turn after half of cooking time.

7. Sprinkle remaining ½ cup (125 mL) mozzarella and ¼ cup (60 mL) Parmesan cheeses on top of cannelloni. Let stand, covered, 3 minutes.

Makes 4 to 6 servings

*For microwave-safe colander, use dishwasher-safe colander with no metal parts.

Tenderloin Diablo

2 pounds (900 g) beef
 tenderloin roast, trimmed
1 small clove garlic, minced
⅛ teaspoon (0.5 mL) black
 pepper
½ teaspoon (2 mL) salt
½ cup (125 mL) butter, at
 room temperature
1 tablespoon (15 mL)
 minced fresh parsley
2 teaspoons (10 mL) minced
 onion
1 teaspoon (5 mL) Dijon-
 style mustard
½ teaspoon (2 mL) drained
 prepared horseradish
Pinch cayenne pepper
Watercress
Cherry tomatoes

1. Rub all surfaces of meat with garlic and black pepper. If one end of roast is tapered, fold it under and tie with

kitchen twine so that roast is uniformly thick. Place on roasting rack in baking dish. Let stand 15 minutes.

2. Place a small piece of aluminum foil over each end of

roast and 1 inch (2.5 cm) down the sides. (Foil shields will reduce meat shrinkage and drying.)

3. Insert microwave-safe thermometer in center of roast. Microwave, uncovered, at High power 3 minutes. Then microwave at Medium (50%) power 5 minutes.

4. Remove foil shields and thermometer; turn roast over. Rotate dish ½ turn; insert thermometer. Microwave, uncovered, at Medium (50%) power until internal temperature reaches 125°F (52°C) for medium rare, 8 to 12 minutes. [For rare, cook to 120°F (49°C), 7 to 10 minutes. For medium, cook to 135°F (57°C), 10 to 16 minutes.]

5. Remove thermometer from roast; sprinkle with salt.

Cover with loose tent of foil, shiny side facing inward. Let stand 10 minutes; temperature will rise about 15°F (8°C).

6. Meanwhile, beat butter in small bowl until creamy. Stir in parsley, onion, mustard, horseradish and cayenne pepper.

7. Transfer roast to serving platter; garnish with watercress and cherry tomatoes. Cut meat into thick slices and serve with seasoned butter.

Makes 6 to 8 servings

Beef and Mushroom Ring

¾ cup (180 mL) water
2 tablespoons (30 mL) butter
  or margarine
2 cups (500 mL) herb-
  seasoned dry stuffing
  mix
1½ pounds (675 g) ground
  beef
2 large eggs
⅓ cup (80 mL) finely
  chopped onion
¼ cup (60 mL) unseasoned
  fine dry bread crumbs
1 tablespoon (15 mL) catsup
1 tablespoon (15 mL)
  minced fresh parsley
1 teaspoon (5 mL)
  Worcestershire sauce
1 teaspoon (5 mL) salt
½ teaspoon (2 mL) dried
  thyme, crumbled
¼ teaspoon (1 mL) pepper
2 cans (4 ounces or 115 g
  each) sliced mushrooms,
  drained
1 medium onion
Parsley sprigs, if desired

1. Place water and butter in medium bowl. Microwave, uncovered, at High power until boiling, 1½ to 2 minutes. Add stuffing mix; mix well.

2. Combine beef, eggs, chopped onion, bread crumbs, catsup, minced parsley, Worcestershire sauce, salt, thyme and pepper in second medium bowl; mix well.

3. Spread 1 can of the mushrooms in even layer in bottom of 6-cup (1.5 L) ring mold. Cut medium onion crosswise into ⅛-inch (0.5 cm) thick slices; separate slices into rings. Arrange onion rings in even layer over mushrooms.

4. Spread ⅓ of the meat mixture evenly over onion rings in mold. Add the remaining can of mushrooms to stuffing mixture; mix well. Spoon ½ of the stuffing mixture in a ring in center of meat layer, leaving 1-inch (2.5 cm) borders around outer edge and center of mold.

5. Top stuffing layer with ⅓ of the meat mixture; spread evenly. Press inner and outer edges firmly with fingers to seal. Make a second layer of stuffing as in Step 4. Top with remaining ⅓ meat mixture and seal edges.

6. Microwave meatloaf, covered with waxed paper, at High power until meat is firm and no longer pink, 8 to 10 minutes; rotate mold ½ turn after about half of cooking time. Let meatloaf stand, covered tightly with aluminum foil, 10 minutes.

7. Drain off any liquid that collects around sides of mold. Unmold meatloaf onto serving dish. Garnish with parsley sprigs. Cut into thick slices or wedges to serve.

Makes 6 servings

Perfect Pepper Steak

1½ pounds (675 g) lean
  boneless beef round
  steak, ½ inch (1.5 cm)
  thick
¼ cup (60 mL) soy sauce
2 teaspoons (10 mL) paprika
2 tablespoons (30 mL)
  vegetable oil
½ cup (125 mL) water
1 medium green bell
  pepper, cut into ¼-inch
  (0.5 mL) strips
1 large stalk celery, cut into
  ¼-inch (0.5 cm) slices
1 small clove garlic, minced
4 green onions, cut into
  ½-inch (1.5 cm) pieces
1 medium tomato, peeled,
  cut into ½-inch (1.5 cm)
  chunks
1½ tablespoons (22 mL)
  cornstarch
3 to 4 cups (750 mL to 1 L)
  hot cooked rice

1. Trim fat from steak. Pound steak with meat mallet or edge of sturdy saucer to about ¼-inch (0.5 cm) thickness. Cut into ¼-inch (0.5 cm) wide strips. Combine beef, soy sauce and paprika in small bowl. Marinate at room temperature 20 minutes.

2. Preheat 10-inch (25 cm) browning dish according to manufacturer's directions. Add oil to dish; swirl to coat.

3. Drain beef; discard marinade. Add beef to hot oil. Microwave, uncovered, at High power until meat is browned, 2 to 3 minutes; stir after about half of cooking time. Add ¼ cup (60 mL) water, the green pepper, celery and garlic to meat.

4. Microwave, covered with lid, at Medium (50%) power until meat is tender and vegetables are crisp-tender, 10 to 14 minutes; stir after about half of cooking time.

5. Add onions and tomato to casserole. Mix cornstarch and the remaining ¼ cup (60 mL) water in cup until smooth. Add to casserole; stir to coat meat and vegetables evenly.

6. Microwave, uncovered, at High power until sauce is thickened, 2 to 4 minutes; stir after about half of cooking time. Serve over hot cooked rice.

Makes 4 to 5 servings

Fish & Seafood

Snappy Salmon Steaks

5 tablespoons (75 mL) butter
  or margarine
2 teaspoons (10 mL) lemon
  juice
3 salmon steaks (1 inch or
  2.5 cm thick), about
  5 ounces or 140 g each
1½ teaspoons (7 mL)
  minced fresh parsley
Pinch dry mustard
Pinch cayenne pepper
Fresh parsley sprigs, if
  desired
Lemon wedges, if desired

1. Microwave butter in custard cup, uncovered, at High power until melted, 45 to 60 seconds. Stir in lemon juice.

2. Arrange salmon steaks evenly spaced in shallow baking dish, leaving about 1-inch space around each steak. Brush top surfaces of salmon with some of the lemon butter.

3. Cover dish with vented plastic wrap. Microwave salmon at High power 2 minutes.

4. Turn salmon steaks over; brush tops lightly with lemon butter. Microwave, covered with vented plastic wrap, at High power just until salmon turns opaque in center, and begins to flake when tested with a fork, 2 to 4 minutes. Let stand, covered, 5 minutes.

5. Microwave remaining lemon butter, uncovered, at High power until hot, 10 to 15 seconds. Stir in minced parsley, mustard and pepper.

6. Transfer salmon to serving platter. Garnish with parsley sprigs and lemon wedges. Spoon lemon-parsley butter over salmon, dividing evenly.

Makes 3 servings

Sole Élégante

3 sole fillets (8 ounces or 225 g each)
1 package (10 ounces or 285 g) frozen chopped spinach
1 package (3 ounces or 85 g) cream cheese
6 tablespoons (90 mL) herb-seasoned stuffing mix
3 tablespoons (45 mL) chopped pecans
1 tablespoon (15 mL) milk
1 tablespoon (15 mL) mayonnaise
¼ teaspoon (1 mL) salt
Paprika
Cherry tomatoes, if desired
Endive, if desired

1. Cut each fillet crosswise into 4 pieces, cut 1 diagonal slit in each of 6 pieces to within ¼ inch (0.5 cm) of corners. Place 1 slit piece on top of each piece without slit to make 6 double-layer pieces. Place in 12×8-inch (30×20 cm) baking dish with thickest portions toward outside of dish.

2. Microwave spinach in package at High power until soft, 3 to 4 minutes; turn package over after about half the time. Place spinach in strainer; press out as much moisture as possible. Discard liquid.

3. Microwave cream cheese in medium bowl, uncovered, at High power until soft, 30 to 45 seconds. Stir in spinach, stuffing mix, pecans, milk, mayonnaise and salt.

4. Spread open slits on top fish pieces to form pockets; stuff each pocket with spinach mixture, dividing evenly. Sprinkle with paprika.

5. Microwave stuffed fillets, covered with waxed paper, at Medium (50%) power until fish flakes and center is set, 15 to 20 minutes; rotate dish ½ turn 2 or 3 times during cooking. Let stand 5 minutes. Serve on endive leaves; garnish with cherry tomatoes.

Makes 6 servings

Butterflied Shrimp with Crab Stuffing

8 fresh jumbo shrimp, in shells
2 tablespoons (30 mL) butter or margarine
4 ounces (115 g) crab meat, rinsed and drained
2 tablespoons (30 mL) fine dry bread crumbs
2 tablespoons (30 mL) minced fresh parsley
2 teaspoons (10 mL) lemon juice
¼ teaspoon (1 mL) salt
Pinch cayenne pepper
Paprika
2 lemon wedges, if desired

1. Loosen shrimp shells at underside of bodies and carefully peel off, leaving tails intact. Make a thin cut down center of back.

2. With tip of knife, loosen and lift out vein. To butterfly shrimp, cut lengthwise, about ⅔ of the way through; spread shrimp flat.

3. Arrange 4 shrimp, cut sides up and tails toward center, in each of 2 small individual casseroles.

4. Microwave butter in medium bowl, uncovered, at High power until melted, 30 to 45 seconds. Flake crab meat, picking out any bits of shell; add to butter. Stir in bread crumbs, parsley, lemon juice, salt and pepper.

5. Spoon about ⅛ of the stuffing in a mound on top of each shrimp. Sprinkle with paprika.

6. Microwave, covered with waxed paper, at Medium (50%) power just until shrimp turn opaque, 5 to 7 minutes; rearrange casseroles twice during cooking. Do not overcook or shrimp will curl up and toughen. Serve with lemon wedges.

Makes 2 servings*

To prepare 4 servings, double all ingredients and prepare as above. Increase cooking time to 11 to 14 minutes; rearrange casseroles 3 times during cooking.

44

Seafood Kabobs

¾ pound (340 g) salmon
   steak (1 inch or 2.5 cm
   thick)
4 small white onions (about
   1 inch or 2.5 cm in
   diameter)
1 small green bell pepper,
   cut into 8 squares
½ pound (225 g) scallops
   (about 1-inch or 2.5 cm
   size)
4 lemon wedges
6 tablespoons (90 mL) butter
   or margarine
3 tablespoons (45 mL) dry
   white wine
½ teaspoon (2 mL) dried
   marjoram leaves, crushed
Pinch black pepper

1. Remove bones and skin from salmon; cut steak into 1-inch (2.5 cm) cubes. Thread each of four 10-inch (25 cm) wooden skewers as follows: Begin with 1 onion and 1 piece green pepper. Then alternate each of 3 scallops and 2 salmon cubes. Finish with 1 piece green pepper and 1 lemon wedge. Place kabobs on roasting rack.

2. Microwave butter, uncovered, in small bowl at High power until melted, 45 to 60 seconds. Whisk in wine, marjoram and black pepper.

Brush kabobs with sauce; cover kabobs with waxed paper.

3. Microwave kabobs at High power until scallops are opaque and flake easily with fork, 3 to 5 minutes; rearrange kabobs and baste with sauce (whisk before each use) 2 or 3 times during cooking.

4. Microwave remaining sauce, uncovered, at High power until heated, 30 to 60 seconds. Serve kabobs with sauce.

Makes 4 servings

Stuffed Sole Provençal

⅓ cup (80 mL) chopped
   onion
⅓ cup (80 mL) chopped
   green bell pepper
1 tablespoon (15 mL) olive
   oil
1 small clove garlic, minced
1 can (6 ounces or 170 g)
   crab meat, rinsed,
   drained and flaked
3 tablespoons (45 mL) fine
   dry bread crumbs
2 tablespoons (30 mL)
   minced fresh parsley
¼ teaspoon (1 mL) lemon
   pepper
Pinch cayenne pepper
2 skinless sole fillets
   (½ pound or 225 g each)
⅓ cup (80 mL) tomato sauce
2 tablespoons (30 mL) dry
   white wine
½ teaspoon (2 mL) dried
   thyme, crumbled
¼ teaspoon (1 mL) dried
   basil, crumbled
¼ teaspoon (1 mL) salt
1 tablespoon (15 mL) butter
3 thick lemon slices, cut in
   half
Parsley sprigs, if desired

1. Combine onion, green pepper, oil and garlic in medium bowl. Microwave, uncovered, at High power until onion and green pepper are tender, 2½ to 3 minutes; stir once during cooking. Stir in crab, bread crumbs, minced parsley, lemon pepper and cayenne pepper.

2. Place one sole fillet on roasting rack. Top with crab stuffing mixture in even layer. Cover with second fillet.

3. Mix tomato sauce, wine, thyme, basil and salt in small bowl. Microwave, uncovered, at High power until bubbly, 1 to 2 minutes. Add butter; stir until melted.

4. Spoon ¼ cup (60 mL) of the sauce over stuffed fish. Arrange lemon half-slices in a row on top of fish.

5. Microwave fish, covered with waxed paper, at Medium (50%) power until bottom fillet is flaky and center of stuffing is hot, 11 to 15 minutes. Rotate roasting rack ½ turn after about half of cooking time.

6. Microwave remaining sauce, uncovered, at High power just until hot, 15 to 30 seconds. Garnish fish with parsley sprigs; serve with remaining sauce.

Makes 3 to 4 servings

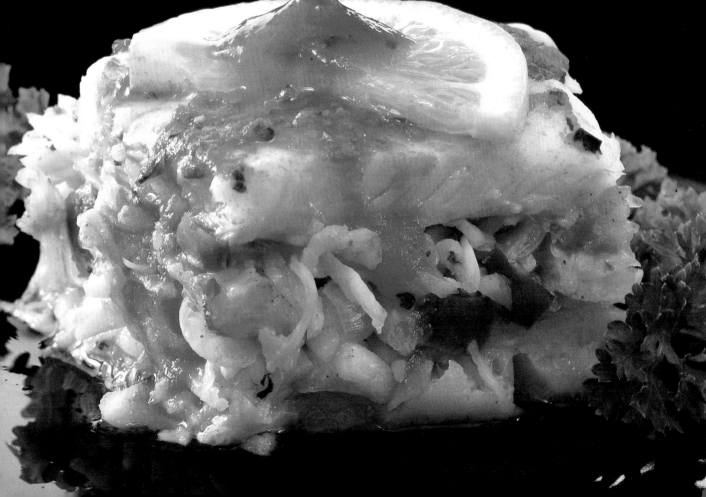

Scallops St. Jacques

1 cup (250 mL) White Sauce (see Index for page number)
2 tablespoons (30 mL) dry white wine
1 pound (450 g) fresh scallops (about 1¼-inch or 3-cm size)
3 tablespoons (45 mL) butter or margarine
⅓ cup (80 mL) fresh bread crumbs
¼ teaspoon (1 mL) dried thyme, crumbled
¼ teaspoon (1 mL) onion salt
3 tablespoons (45 mL) grated Parmesan cheese
1 teaspoon (5 mL) minced fresh parsley

1. Prepare White Sauce. Stir in wine. Reserve.

2. Rinse scallops in colander under cold running water. Drain well; pat dry. Arrange scallops in single layer in 8×8-inch (20×20 cm) dish.

3. Microwave scallops, covered with vented plastic wrap, at High power just until opaque, 3½ to 4½ minutes.

Stir to rearrange scallops once during cooking.

4. Let scallops stand, covered, 1 minute. (Cut 1 scallop in half; center should be opaque and flaky but moist.) Drain scallops. Mix scallops with White Sauce; spoon into 4 ramekins or large scallop shells.

5. Microwave butter in small bowl, uncovered, at High power until melted, 30 to 45 seconds. Add bread crumbs, thyme and onion salt; stir and toss until crumbs are evenly moistened. Microwave at High power 1 minute, stirring once. Stir in cheese and parsley.

6. Sprinkle crumb mixture evenly over scallops. Microwave, uncovered, at High power until hot, 1½ to 2½ minutes; rearrange ramekins after about half of cooking time.

Makes 4 servings

Fillets Almondine

5 tablespoons (75 mL) butter or margarine
⅓ cup (80 mL) slivered blanched almonds
1½ pounds (675 g) skinless fresh sole or flounder fillets
2 tablespoons (30 mL) dry white wine
¼ teaspoon (1 mL) salt
Fresh parsley sprigs, if desired
Lemon wedges, if desired

1. Microwave butter in 1-cup (250 mL) measure, uncovered, at High power until melted, 45 to 60 seconds. Place 1 tablespoon (15 mL) of the melted butter in 9-inch (23 cm) pie plate; reserve remaining butter.

2. Add almonds to pie plate. Stir and toss until evenly coated with butter. Microwave, uncovered, at High power until almonds are pale golden, 2½ to 4½ minutes; stir almonds every 2 minutes during cooking. Let almonds stand, uncovered, 5 minutes; almonds will continue to cook and color will darken on standing. Reserve.

3. Arrange fish fillets in 13×9-inch (33×23 cm) baking dish placing thickest portions toward the outside and overlapping thin portions at center of dish.

4. Drizzle wine over fish; sprinkle with salt. Pour the reserved butter over fish. Cover dish with vented plastic wrap. Microwave at High power 3½ minutes. Rotate dish ½ turn.

5. With a fork, carefully reverse order of the overlapping thin portions at center. Microwave, covered with vented plastic wrap, at High power just until fish turns opaque and begins to flake when tested with a fork, 4 to 7 minutes.

6. Using broad spatula, carefully transfer fillets to serving platter; spoon cooking juices over fish. Garnish with parsley and lemon wedges. Sprinkle with almonds.

Makes 4 servings

Family Favorites

Burgers Deluxe

6 slices bacon
1 tablespoon (15 mL)
   browning sauce
1 tablespoon (15 mL) water
1 pound (450 g) ground beef
4 slices American cheese
8 slices dill pickle
4 sesame seed buns, split
Green onions, if desired

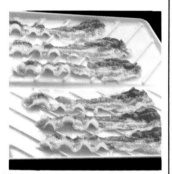

1. Arrange bacon in single layer on roasting rack or on a rack placed in baking dish. Microwave, covered with paper toweling, at High power until slightly underdone, 4½ to 6 minutes (45 to 60 seconds per slice). Bacon fat will be bubbly and still slightly translucent. Let stand, covered, 5 minutes to complete cooking.

2. Mix browning sauce with water in a cup. Shape beef into 4 even patties, each ½-inch (1.5 cm) thick; arrange evenly spaced on roasting rack. Brush tops and sides with sauce mixture. Microwave, covered with waxed paper, at High power 2 minutes. Turn patties over; brush with sauce mixture. Microwave, covered, at High power until done slightly less than desired, 1½ to 2½ minutes.*

3. Top each burger with 1½ slices bacon and 1 slice cheese. Let stand, loosely covered, 1 to 2 minutes. (Cheese should melt slightly during standing time. If necessary, microwave, uncovered, at High power 15 to 45 seconds.) Top burgers with pickle slices. Place in buns and serve, garnished with green onions.

Makes 4 servings

Cooking times given are for medium-done burgers; for rare or well-done burgers, decrease or increase cooking times by about ½ minute.

Fiesta Tamales

1 quart (1 L) plus
  1 teaspoon (5 mL) water
4 dried corn husks

FILLING
¼ pound (115 g) pork loin,
  cut into thin strips
1 medium tomato, seeded
  and chopped
¼ cup (60 mL) chopped
  onion
1 clove garlic, lightly
  crushed
2 tablespoons (30 mL)
  chopped canned green
  chilies
2 tablespoons (30 mL)
  catsup
½ teaspoon (2 mL) chili
  powder
⅛ teaspoon (0.5 mL) salt

DOUGH
1 ounce (30 g) cream cheese
3 tablespoons (45 mL) butter
½ cup (125 mL) yellow
  cornmeal
½ teaspoon (2 mL) baking
  powder
1 egg, lightly beaten
1 tablespoon (15 mL) honey

1. Microwave 1 quart (1 L) water in large bowl, covered with plastic wrap, at High power until boiling, 8 to 10 minutes. Add corn husks to water. Let stand, covered, to soften.

2. For Filling: Combine pork, tomato, onion and garlic in small bowl. Microwave, uncovered, at Medium (50%) power until pork is no longer pink, 4 to 6 minutes; stir every 2 minutes during cooking. Drain well.

3. Add remaining filling ingredients to pork mixture; stir to mix well. Microwave, uncovered, at Medium (50%) power until pork is tender and flavors are blended, 4 to 6 minutes; stir after about half of cooking time. Discard garlic. Reserve filling.

4. For Dough: Microwave cream cheese in custard cup, uncovered, at Medium (50%) power until softened, 15 to 30 seconds.

5. Microwave butter in 2-cup (500 mL) measure, uncovered, at High power until melted, 30 to 45 seconds. Add cream cheese and remaining dough ingredients; stir until dough is smooth.

6. Remove corn husks from water; pat dry. Cut 2 strips (¼ inch or 0.5 cm wide) lengthwise from each corn husk; reserve. Spread ¼ of the dough in thin layer in center of each husk. Top each with ¼ of the filling; spread to within ¼ inch (0.5 cm) of dough edges.

Roll sides of husks around filling; fold ends over. Tie ends securely with corn-husk strips or kitchen string.

7. Place tamales in single layer in 8×8-inch (20×20 cm) baking dish; add 1 teaspoon (5 mL) water to dish. Microwave, covered with plastic wrap, at Medium (50%) power until firm to the touch, 3 to 6 minutes; turn tamales over and rotate dish ½ turn after about half of cooking time.

Makes 4 tamales

Mexicali Casserole

2 tablespoons (30 mL) butter
  or margarine
1 medium onion, chopped
1 large green bell pepper,
  chopped
1 can (4 ounces or 115 g)
  diced green chilies,
  drained
3 large eggs
1 cup (250 mL) small-curd
  creamed cottage cheese
1 teaspoon (5 mL) chili
  powder
½ teaspoon (2 mL) salt
½ teaspoon (2mL) dried
  oregano, crumbled
¼ teaspoon (1 mL) ground
  cumin
4 cups (1 L) coarsely
  crushed tortilla chips
2 cups (500 mL) shredded
  Monterey Jack cheese
1½ cups (375 mL) shredded
  Cheddar cheese
1 cup (250 mL) sour cream

1. Microwave butter in medium bowl, uncovered, at High power until melted, 30

to 45 seconds. Stir in onion and bell pepper. Microwave, uncovered, at High power until onion and pepper are tender, 3 to 5 minutes; stir after about half of cooking time. Stir in green chilies; reserve.

2. Whisk eggs in 4-cup (1 L) measure. Whisk in cottage cheese, chili powder, salt, oregano and cumin.

3. Spread 1½ cups (375 mL) tortilla chips in even layer in bottom of 12×8-inch (30×20 cm) baking dish. Proceed

with layers in order as follows: ½ the egg mixture; ½ the onion mixture; 1½ cups (375 mL) Jack cheese; 1 cup (250 mL) Cheddar cheese; 1½ cups (375 mL) tortilla chips; remaining egg mixture; and top with remaining onion mixture.

4. Microwave casserole, uncovered, at High power 5 minutes. Microwave, uncovered, at Medium (50%) power until center is almost set, 9 to 14 minutes; rotate dish ½ turn after about half of cooking time.

5. Mix sour cream and remaining ½ cup (125 mL) each Jack and Cheddar cheeses in medium bowl; spread evenly on casserole. Sprinkle with the remaining 1 cup (250 mL) tortilla chips.

6. Microwave casserole, uncovered, at High power until sour cream mixture is hot, 3 to 5 minutes; rotate dish ½ turn after about half of cooking time. Let stand, uncovered, 3 minutes before serving.

Makes 4 to 6 servings

Festive Chili Con Carne

1 pound (450 g) ground beef
  or pork
1 medium onion, chopped
1 medium green bell
  pepper, chopped
1 clove garlic, minced
2 to 4 teaspoons (10 to
  20 mL) chili powder
1 teaspoon (5 mL) salt
½ teaspoon (2 mL) dried
  oregano, crumbled
1 can (1 pound or 450 g)
  whole tomatoes,
  undrained
1 can (8 ounces or 225 g)
  tomato sauce
1 can (15 ounces or 425 g)
  red kidney beans,
  drained
1 tablespoon (15 mL) red
  wine vinegar
Tortilla chips or crackers

1. Crumble meat into microwave-safe plastic colander.* Place colander in 2-quart (2 L) casserole. Microwave, uncovered, at High power until meat is no longer pink, 4 to 6 minutes; stir with fork to break up meat every 2 minutes during cooking.

2. Discard meat drippings from casserole. Transfer meat from colander to casserole; break up into small pieces with back of spoon. Stir in onion, green pepper and garlic. Microwave, uncovered, at High power until onion and pepper are tender, 4 to 5 minutes.

3. Add chili powder, salt and oregano to casserole; mix well. Drain tomato liquid into casserole. Chop tomatoes in can with scissors or knife; add to casserole. Add tomato

sauce and beans; mix well. Microwave, covered with lid, at High power 5 minutes.

4. Add vinegar to chili; stir to mix well. Microwave, uncovered, at Medium (50%) power 20 to 25 minutes until slightly thickened and to allow flavors to blend; stir twice during cooking. Serve with chips or crackers.

Makes 4 servings

For microwave-safe colander, use dishwasher-safe plastic colander with no metal parts.

Lasagne Vegetali

6 ounces (170 g) fresh
  mushrooms, coarsely
  chopped
1 medium green bell
  pepper, chopped
⅔ cup (160 mL) chopped
  zucchini
½ cup (125 mL) chopped
  onion
1 clove garlic, minced
2 tablespoons (30 mL) olive
  oil
1 can (16 ounces or 450 g)
  whole tomatoes
1 can (12 ounces or 340 g)
  tomato paste
⅓ cup (80 mL) dry red wine
  or water
3 tablespoons (45 mL)
  minced fresh parsley
2 teaspoons (10 mL) sugar
1 teaspoon (5 mL) salt
1 teaspoon (5 mL) dried
  basil
1 teaspoon (5 mL) dried
  oregano
2 bay leaves
1 container (15 ounces or
  425 g) ricotta cheese,
  drained
2 large eggs, lightly beaten

½ cup (125 mL) grated
  Parmesan cheese
⅛ teaspoon (0.5 mL) black
  pepper
9 lasagne noodles, cooked
  and drained
3 cups (750 mL) shredded
  mozzarella cheese

1. Combine mushrooms, green pepper, zucchini, onion, garlic and oil in 3-quart (3 L) casserole; mix well. Microwave, covered with plastic wrap, at High power until vegetables are tender, 4 to 6 minutes; stir after about half of cooking time.

2. Add tomatoes, tomato paste, wine, parsley, sugar, salt, basil, oregano and bay leaves to casserole; stir to mix well. Microwave, uncovered, at High power 5 minutes. Stir mixture, breaking up tomatoes with spoon.

3. Microwave tomato mixture, uncovered, at Medium (50%) power until sauce is thickened and flavors are blended, 20 to 25 minutes; stir sauce every 7 minutes during cooking. Discard bay leaves.

4. Combine ricotta cheese, eggs, ¼ cup (60 mL) Parmesan cheese and the black pepper in medium bowl; mix well.

5. To assemble lasagne, cover bottom of 12×8-inch (30×20 cm) baking dish with 3 of the lasagne noodles; top with ⅓

each of the ricotta mixture, sauce and mozzarella in that order. Repeat all layers 2 more times. Sprinkle remaining ¼ cup (60 mL) Parmesan cheese over top.

6. Microwave lasagne, uncovered, at Medium (50%) power until hot in center and bubbly around edges, about 20 minutes; rotate dish ½ turn after about half of cooking time. Let stand, uncovered, 10 minutes to set before serving.

Makes 8 servings

Mushroom Quiche

CRUST

1 cup (250 mL) all-purpose
  flour
½ teaspoon (2 mL) salt
¼ cup (60 mL) solid
  vegetable shortening
3 tablespoons (45 mL) butter
  or margarine, at room
  temperature
2 tablespoons (30 mL) cold
  water

FILLING

12 ounces (340 g) fresh
  mushrooms, sliced
3 large eggs
¾ cup (180 mL) light cream
  or half-and-half
⅓ cup (80 mL) chopped
  green onion
2 teaspoons (10 mL) finely
  chopped fresh parsley
¼ teaspoon (1 mL) dry
  mustard
¼ teaspoon (1 mL) salt
¼ teaspoon (1 mL) pepper

1. For Crust: Measure flour and salt into medium bowl; stir to mix. Cut shortening and butter into flour with pastry blender or 2 knives until mixture resembles coarse crumbs. Gradually stir in water with fork just until mixture is evenly moistened. Spread mixture in 9-inch (23 cm) pie plate; press evenly with fingers over bottom and sides of plate to form crust.

2. Microwave crust, uncovered, at High power until bottom appears dry, 4 to 5 minutes; rotate plate ½ turn after 2 minutes of cooking. Reserve.

3. For Filling: Place mushrooms in 1½-quart (1.5 L) casserole. Microwave, uncovered, at High power until mushrooms are tender, 5 to 7 minutes; stir once during cooking. Drain and pat dry on paper toweling. Spread mushrooms in reserved crust.

4. Place eggs, cream, onion, parsley, mustard, salt and pepper in 1½-quart (1.5 L) casserole; mix well with whisk. Microwave, uncovered, at Medium (50%) power until hot but not set, 1½ to 2 minutes; stir mixture every 30 seconds.

5. Pour egg mixture over mushrooms in crust. Microwave, uncovered, at Medium (50%) power until soft set in center, 7 to 11 minutes; rotate quiche ½ turn every 3 minutes. Let stand 5 minutes to complete cooking.

Makes 4 servings

Shrimp & Egg Foo Yung

6 ounces (170 g) frozen, cooked, tiny shrimp
1 cup (250 mL) water
1 tablespoon (15 mL) cornstarch
1 tablespoon (15 mL) soy sauce
2 teaspoons (10 mL) instant chicken bouillon granules
1 teaspoon (5 mL) sugar
Pinch ground ginger
1 tablespoon (15 mL) butter or margarine
3 green onions, thinly sliced
½ medium green bell pepper, chopped
6 large eggs, well beaten
1 can (16 ounces or 450 g) bean sprouts, drained
¼ teaspoon (1 mL) salt

1. To Defrost Shrimp: Spread frozen shrimp in single layer in 13×9-inch (33×23 cm) dish. Microwave, uncovered, at Medium (50%) power just until soft, 2 to 3 minutes; stir to break up shrimp after 1 minute. Rinse under cold running water; drain well.

2. Place ¼ cup (60 mL) of the water and the cornstarch in 1-quart (1 L) casserole; stir until smooth. Stir in remaining ¾ cup (180 mL) water, the soy sauce, bouillon granules, sugar and ginger. Microwave, uncovered, at High power until thickened and smooth, 4 to 5 minutes; stir twice during cooking. Reserve sauce.

3. Place butter, onions and green pepper in 2-quart (2 L) casserole. Microwave, uncovered, at High power until green pepper is crisp-tender, 3 to 4 minutes; stir after about half of cooking time.

4. Add shrimp, beaten eggs, bean sprouts and salt to green-pepper mixture; mix well. Microwave, uncovered, at High power 3 minutes. Stir to break up; push cooked portions to center.

5. Microwave egg mixture, uncovered, at Medium (50%) power until eggs are set, 6 to 8 minutes; stir twice during cooking. To serve, pour reserved sauce over eggs.

Makes 4 servings

Fluffy Omelet

4 large eggs, separated, at room temperature
¼ cup (60 mL) milk or cream
½ teaspoon (2 mL) salt
¼ teaspoon (1 mL) baking powder
⅛ teaspoon (0.5 mL) black pepper
1 tablespoon (15 mL) butter or margarine
¼ cup (60 mL) chopped tomato
¼ cup (60 mL) chopped green bell pepper
2 tablespoons (30 mL) chopped onion

1. Beat egg whites in large mixer bowl just until stiff peaks form. Beat egg yolks, milk, salt, baking powder and black pepper in small bowl until well blended. Gently fold egg yolk mixture into egg whites until no streaks of white remain.

2. Microwave butter in 9-inch (23 cm) pie plate, uncovered, at High power until melted, 15 to 30 seconds. Add egg mixture; spread in even layer. Microwave, uncovered, at Medium (50%) power until eggs are partially set, 3 to 5 minutes.

3. Lift edges of eggs with rubber spatula to spread and distribute uncooked portion evenly. Microwave, uncovered, at Medium (50%) power until eggs are almost set in center, 2 to 4 minutes.

4. Sprinkle tomato, green pepper and onion evenly on one half of the omelet. (Reserve some vegetables to sprinkle on top of omelet, if desired.) Gently loosen omelet with spatula; fold in half. Slide gently onto plate.

Makes 2 servings

Variation: Shredded cheese, chopped ham, sautéed mushrooms, crumbled cooked bacon or other ingredients of your choice can be substituted for the tomato, green pepper and onion.

Country-Style Omelet

½ pound (225 g) ground
   pork sausage
1 medium onion, chopped
2 cups (500 mL) shredded
   potatoes
¾ teaspoon (4 mL) salt
6 large eggs, lightly beaten
¼ cup (60 mL) milk
⅛ teaspoon (0.5 mL) black
   pepper
Pinch cayenne pepper
¼ teaspoon (1 mL) dried
   thyme
⅛ teaspoon (0.5 mL) ground
   sage

1. Crumble sausage into shallow 2-quart (2 L) casserole; add onion. Microwave, uncovered, at High power until sausage is no longer pink, 3½ to 5 minutes; stir twice during cooking, breaking sausage into small pieces.

2. Remove sausage and onion from casserole with slotted spoon; drain on paper toweling. Remove and discard all but 1 tablespoon (15 mL) drippings from casserole.

3. Add potatoes to casserole. Microwave, covered, at High power until potatoes are tender, 4 to 6 minutes. Stir in ¼ teaspoon (1 mL) of the salt; spread potatoes in even layer.

4. Mix eggs, milk, the remaining ½ teaspoon (2 mL) salt, the black pepper and cayenne pepper in 2-cup (500 mL) measure; pour evenly over potatoes in casserole. Mix sausage mixture with thyme and sage in small bowl; sprinkle evenly over potatoes.

5. Microwave omelet, uncovered, at High power 3 min-

utes. Lift edges of omelet with rubber spatula to spread and distribute uncooked portion of egg mixture evenly. (Take care not to disturb potato and meat layers.)

6. Microwave omelet, uncovered, at Medium (50%) power until eggs are almost set, 8 to 12 minutes; rotate casserole ¼ turn twice during cooking. Let omelet stand, loosely covered with aluminum foil, 2 minutes before serving.

Makes 4 servings

Golden Cheese Soufflé

¼ cup (60 mL) butter or
   margarine
¼ cup (60 mL) all-purpose
   flour
1 teaspoon (5 mL) salt
Pinch cayenne pepper
1 can (13 fluid ounces or
   400 mL) evaporated milk
1 cup (250 mL) shredded
   Cheddar cheese
6 large eggs, at room
   temperature, separated
1 tablespoon (15 mL) finely
   chopped fresh parsley
½ teaspoon (2 mL) dried
   basil leaves, crushed
1 teaspoon (5 mL) cream of
   tartar

1. Microwave butter, uncovered, in 1½-quart (1.5 L) casserole at High power until melted, 1 to 1¼ minutes. Stir in flour, salt and pepper until smooth. Stir in milk with wire whisk.

2. Microwave milk mixture, uncovered, at High power until sauce is smooth and thickened, 4 to 5 minutes; stir after first 2 minutes and then every minute. Add cheese; stir until melted.

3. Beat egg yolks lightly in small bowl; stir small amount of hot sauce into yolks. Pour egg-yolk mixture into remaining sauce, stirring rapidly to prevent lumps. Mix in parsley and basil. Reserve.

4. Beat egg whites and cream of tartar in large bowl until stiff peaks form. Fold cheese mixture gently into egg whites using rubber spatula. Pour mixture into 2-quart (2 L) soufflé dish.

5. Microwave, uncovered, at Medium-Low (30%) power until top is almost dry, 25 to 30 minutes. Rotate dish as needed: Soufflé may rise faster on 1 side. If so, rotate dish so that low part is positioned in the oven area where the higher part of the soufflé was prior to rotating.

6. To be sure soufflé evens out during microwaving, check on it every 5 or 6 minutes. Number of times needed to rotate dish depends upon the oven's specific cooking pattern. Serve immediately when cooking is completed.

Makes 6 servings

Breads

Apple Breakfast Round

1 recipe Rich Dough (recipe follows)
3 tablespoons (45 mL) butter or margarine
⅓ cup (80 mL) granulated sugar
⅓ cup (80 mL) packed brown sugar
⅓ cup (80 mL) graham cracker or vanilla wafer crumbs
2 teaspoons (10 mL) ground cinnamon
¼ teaspoon (1 mL) ground nutmeg
2 tart medium apples

1. Prepare Rich Dough.

2. Microwave butter in custard cup, uncovered, at High power until melted, 30 to 45 seconds; cool slightly.

3. Mix granulated and brown sugars, crumbs, cinnamon and nutmeg in small bowl. Pare and core apples; cut each lengthwise into 12 slices. Cut dough into quarters; cut each quarter into 6 pieces.

4. Dip dough pieces in butter and then in crumb mixture to coat evenly. Arrange in a layer, alternating with apple slices, in bottom of 10- or 12-cup (2.5 or 3 L) microwave-safe tube cake dish. Top with second layer of dough and apple pieces.

5. Raise dough in microwave oven, following procedure in Step 4 of "German Pumpernickel Ring" (page 66) until light and doubled in size.

6. Sprinkle cake with any remaining crumb mixture. Microwave, uncovered, at Medium (50%) power 6 minutes; rotate dish ¼ turn every 3 minutes during cooking.

7. Microwave, uncovered, at High power until top springs back when pressed lightly in several places, 30 seconds to 5 minutes; rotate dish ¼ turn every 2 minutes during cooking.

8. Let cake stand, uncovered, 2 minutes. Loosen edges; invert onto serving dish. Serve warm as pull-apart ring or cool and cut into slices.

Makes 1 coffeecake

Rich Dough

1 package (¼ ounce or 7 g) active dry yeast
¼ cup (60 mL) very warm water (105°F to 115°F or 40°C to 46°C)
¼ cup (60 mL) butter or margarine
½ cup (125 mL) milk, at room temperature
1 large egg, at room temperature
2 tablespoons (30 mL) sugar
1 teaspoon (5 mL) salt
2½ to 3 cups (625 to 750 mL) all-purpose flour

1. Sprinkle yeast over very warm water in a cup or small bowl. Stir until yeast is dissolved.

2. Microwave butter in large bowl, uncovered, at High power just until melted, 45 to 60 seconds. Whisk in milk, egg, sugar, and salt. Stir in yeast mixture. Add flour, ½ cup (125 mL) at a time, beating well after each addition; use as much of the flour as needed to form stiff dough.

3. Knead dough on well-floured surface until smooth, elastic and no longer sticky, about 10 minutes; add as much of the remaining flour to surface as needed to prevent sticking during kneading. (Properly kneaded dough will feel smooth and satiny and have a layer of tiny bubbles visible just below the surface.)

4. Shape dough into ball; place in large greased bowl, turning dough over to grease all sides.

5. To raise dough in microwave oven, follow directions in Step 4 of "German Pumpernickel Ring" (page 66) until light and doubled in size. (To test for doubling, quickly press 2 fingers 1 inch (2.5 cm) into dough about midway between center and edge of bowl. If impressions remain, dough is doubled. If dough springs back and impressions fill in, dough needs further rising.)

6. Punch down dough; knead briefly. Shape into ball; let rest, covered with inverted bowl, 5 to 10 minutes.

Orange-Bran Muffins

⅓ cup (80 mL) solid
    vegetable shortening
1 cup (250 mL) bran flakes
⅔ cup (160 mL) milk
1 cup (250 mL) all-purpose
    flour
2 tablespoons (30 mL) sugar
1½ teaspoons (7 mL) baking
    powder
1½ teaspoons (7 mL) grated
    orange rind
¼ teaspoon (1 mL) salt
¼ cup (60 mL) molasses
1 large egg
¼ cup (60 mL) raisins, if
    desired

1. Line each of 6 custard cups or microwave muffin-ring cups with 2 paper cupcake liners.*

2. Microwave shortening in small bowl, uncovered, at High power until melted, 1 to 1¼ minutes.

3. Place bran flakes in large bowl. Add remaining ingredients except shortening, in order given. Add shortening and stir just until dry ingredients are moistened; do not overmix batter.

4. Spoon batter into prepared cups, filling paper liners half full.

5. Arrange custard cups in a circle in microwave oven.

Microwave, uncovered, at High power until tops are mostly dry with only a few moist spots and centers are just firm to the touch, 2½ to 4 minutes; rearrange cups and rotate ½ turn after about half of cooking time. (If using muffin-ring, rotate ring ½ turn.) Immediately remove muffins from cups to wire rack. Let stand until moist spots have dried.

6. Repeat Steps 1 and 5, using remaining batter. For 4 to 5 muffins, decrease microwaving time to 1½ to 2½ minutes.

Makes 10 to 12 muffins

If microwaving less than 6 muffins in muffin-ring, alternate cups to allow for more even cooking.

Banana-Nut Loaf

1½ cups (375 mL) all-
    purpose flour
¾ cup (180 mL) sugar
½ cup (125 mL) plus
    2 tablespoons (30 mL)
    butter or margarine, cut
    into 10 pieces, at room
    temperature
⅓ cup (80 mL) milk
2 large eggs
2 ripe medium bananas,
    sliced
1 tablespoon (15 mL) lemon
    juice
¾ teaspoon (4 mL) grated
    lemon rind
1 teaspoon (5 mL) baking
    soda
½ teaspoon (2 mL) salt
¼ teaspoon (1 mL) ground
    nutmeg
½ cup (125 mL) chopped
    walnuts or pecans

1. Place flour in large mixer bowl. Add remaining ingredients except ¼ cup (60 mL) of the walnuts. Beat mixture at low speed until blended; then beat at high speed 2 minutes.

2. Line bottom of 9×5×3-inch (23×13×8 cm) loaf dish with waxed paper. Pour batter into dish; spread top smooth. Sprinkle with remaining ¼ cup (60 mL) walnuts.

3. Wrap one 8×2-inch (20×5 cm) strip of aluminum foil

around each end of loaf dish so that 1 inch (2.5 cm) of batter is shielded with foil.

4. Place inverted saucer in microwave oven; center loaf dish on saucer. Microwave,

uncovered, at Medium (50%) power 9 minutes; rotate dish ¼ turn every 3 minutes.

5. Microwave, uncovered, at High power until center springs back when lightly pressed and no unbaked batter is visible through bottom of dish, 4 to 7 minutes; remove foil shields and rotate dish ¼ turn after 2 minutes. Let stand directly on heat-proof surface, uncovered, 5 to 10 minutes. Remove bread from dish; cool completely on wire rack.

Makes 1 loaf

German Pumpernickel Ring

¼ cup (60 mL) solid
    vegetable shortening
1 package (¼ ounce or 7 g)
    active dry yeast
½ cup (125 mL) very warm
    water (105°F to 115°F or
    40°C to 46°C)
1 cup (250 mL) mashed
    potatoes, at room
    temperature
½ cup (125 mL) molasses
1½ teaspoons (7 mL)
    caraway seeds
1 teaspoon (5 mL) salt
1 cup (250 mL) rye flour
1 cup (250 mL) plus
    3 tablespoons (45 mL)
    whole wheat flour
2 teaspoons (10 mL)
    unsweetened cocoa
    powder
1 to 1½ cups (250 to
    375 mL) all-purpose flour
3 tablespoons (45 mL)
    cornmeal
1 tablespoon (15 mL) butter

1. Microwave shortening in small bowl, uncovered, at High power until melted, 45 to 60 seconds; cool slightly.

2. Sprinkle yeast over water in large bowl; stir until yeast is dissolved. Stir in potatoes, molasses, caraway seeds and salt. Stir in shortening.

3. Mix rye flour, 1 cup (250 mL) whole wheat flour and the cocoa in medium bowl; add to yeast mixture and mix well. Stir in as much of the all-purpose flour needed to make a very stiff dough. Knead, using remaining all-purpose flour, until smooth and elastic. Shape into ball; place in large greased bowl, turning dough to grease all sides.

4. To raise dough in microwave oven, cover bowl with waxed paper; place in dish of hot water. Microwave at Low (30%) power 1 minute; let stand 15 minutes. [If oven has uneven pattern, microwave at Warm (10%) power 4 minutes; let stand 15 minutes.] Rotate dish ¼ turn. Repeat microwaving, standing and rotating sequence as many times as needed until dough is light and almost doubled in size.

5. Punch down dough; knead briefly. Shape into ball; cover with inverted bowl. Let rest 15 minutes.

6. Mix cornmeal and remaining 3 tablespoons (45 mL) whole wheat flour in small bowl. Sprinkle about ⅓ of the cornmeal mixture in well-greased 10-inch (25 cm) pie plate or on microwave-safe baking sheet; shake to coat evenly. Microwave butter in custard cup, uncovered, at High power until melted, 15 to 30 seconds.

7. Roll dough on board into 15-inch (38 cm) long strip. Brush all surfaces with butter; coat evenly with remaining cornmeal mixture. Shape into a ring, pinching ends together to seal. Place in prepared pie plate. Insert greased

microwave-safe glass, open-end-up, into center of ring.

8. Raise dough in microwave oven, following procedure in Step 4, until light and almost doubled. Remove dish of water and waxed paper.

9. Microwave bread, uncovered, at Medium (50%) power 6 minutes; rotate ¼ turn every 3 minutes. Microwave at High power until top springs back when pressed lightly in several places, 2 to 6 minutes; rotate ¼ turn every 2 minutes. Let stand, uncovered, 10 minutes. Remove glass. Remove bread from pie plate; cool on wire rack.

Makes 1 ring loaf

White Sauce

2 tablespoons (30 mL) butter
  or margarine
2 tablespoons (30 mL) all-
  purpose flour
¼ teaspoon (1 mL) salt
Pinch white pepper
1 cup (250 mL) milk

1. Place butter in 4-cup (1 L) measure. Microwave, un-covered, at High power until butter is melted, 30 to 45 seconds.

2. Add flour, salt and pepper to butter; stir until smooth. Gradually stir in milk until smooth.

3. Microwave milk mixture, uncovered, at High power until sauce thickens and coats a spoon, 6 to 8 minutes; stir sauce after each minute during cooking.

Makes about 1 cup (250 mL)

Cheese Sauce Variation:
Prepare White Sauce as above. Add ½ cup (125 mL) shredded American, Cheddar or Swiss cheese; stir until cheese melts and sauce is smooth.

Hollandaise Sauce

3 large egg yolks
2 tablespoons (30 mL) fresh
  lemon juice
¼ teaspoon (1 mL) salt
Pinch cayenne pepper
½ cup (125 mL) butter or
  margarine

1. Whisk egg yolks, lemon juice, salt and pepper in small bowl until blended.

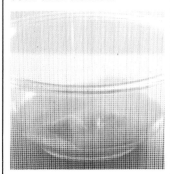

2. Cut butter into 6 to 8 pieces. Microwave in medium bowl, uncovered, at High power until melted but not bubbling hot, 45 seconds to 1¼ minutes.

3. Whisk egg yolk mixture in-to butter; whisk briskly until thoroughly blended.

4. Microwave, uncovered, at Medium (50%) power until sauce is thickened, 45 seconds to 1¾ minutes; whisk every 30 seconds during cooking. (Watch carefully as sauce be-gins to thicken; sauce will cur-dle if overcooked.) Whisk sauce briskly before serving. Serve over vegetables.

Makes about ¾ cup (180 mL)

Layered Asparagus Casserole

2 pounds (900 g) fresh
  asparagus, cut into
  1½-inch (4 cm) lengths*
¼ cup (60 mL) water
3 tablespoons (45 mL) butter
  or margarine
¼ cup (60 mL) fine dry
  bread crumbs
⅛ teaspoon (0.5 mL)
  paprika
⅓ cup (80 mL) cashews
2 tablespoons (30 mL) all-
  purpose flour
¼ teaspoon (1 mL) celery
  salt
¼ teaspoon (1 mL) dry
  mustard
⅛ teaspoon (0.5 mL) garlic
  powder
⅛ teaspoon (0.5 mL) pepper
1 cup (250 mL) milk
1 cup (250 mL) coarsely
  shredded mild or
  medium-sharp Cheddar
  cheese

*Two packages (8 ounces or 225 g
each) frozen cut asparagus can be
substituted for fresh. Decrease
water to 2 tablespoons (30 mL).*

1. Place asparagus and water in 1½-quart (1.5 L) casserole. Microwave, covered with lid, at High power just until crisp-tender, 8 to 12 minutes; stir after about half of cooking time. Drain asparagus.

2. Microwave 1 tablespoon (15 mL) of the butter in small bowl, uncovered, at High power until melted, 15 to 30 seconds. Add bread crumbs and paprika; stir and toss with fork until crumbs are evenly moistened. Stir in cashews.

3. Microwave remaining 2 tablespoons (30 mL) butter in 4-cup (1 L) measure, uncovered, at High power until melted, 30 to 45 seconds. Add flour, celery salt, mustard, garlic powder and pepper; stir until smooth. Add milk and stir until smooth.

4. Microwave milk mixture, uncovered, at High power until sauce is thickened and bubbly, 5 to 7 minutes; stir sauce after each minute during cooking.

5. Place ½ of the asparagus in bottom of the 1½-quart (1.5 L) casserole. Pour ½ of the sauce over asparagus; sprinkle with ½ of the cheese. Repeat layers with remaining asparagus, sauce and cheese.

6. Sprinkle crumb mixture evenly over top of casserole. Microwave, uncovered, at High power until hot and bubbly, 3 to 5 minutes; rotate casserole ½ turn after about half of cooking time.

Makes 6 to 8 servings

Double Potato Bake

6 slices bacon
3 large baking potatoes,
   scrubbed
3 tablespoons (45 mL) butter
   or margarine
3 green onions, thinly sliced
⅓ cup (80 mL) milk
½ teaspoon (2 mL) salt
⅛ teaspoon (0.5 mL) pepper
3 tablespoons (45 mL)
   grated Parmesan cheese
Paprika

1. Arrange bacon in single layer on roasting rack or on a rack placed in baking dish. Microwave, covered with paper toweling, at High power until slightly underdone, 4½ to 6 minutes (45 to 60 seconds per slice). Bacon fat will be bubbly and still slightly translucent. Let stand, covered, 5 minutes to complete cooking.

2. Pierce each potato in 2 places with fork. Arrange in star shape in microwave oven on layer of paper toweling, leaving 1 inch (2.5 cm) space between potatoes.

3. Microwave potatoes, uncovered, at High power until they can be pierced to the center with fork but are still slightly firm, 8½ to 11½ minutes. Rearrange potatoes and turn them over after about half of cooking time.

Place potatoes on counter; cover with bowl or wrap in foil. Let stand 5 to 10 minutes.

4. Combine butter and 2 of the onions in 2-quart (2 L) casserole. Microwave, covered with lid, at High power until butter is melted and onions are soft, 1½ to 2 minutes.

5. Cut potatoes horizontally in half. Scoop out centers of potatoes and add to butter in casserole; reserve potato skins. Mash potatoes. Add milk, salt and pepper; mash until potatoes are fluffy. Finely crumble bacon; add bacon and cheese to potatoes and mix well. Spoon mixture into potato-skin shells, dividing evenly.

6. Arrange potatoes, evenly spaced, on baking sheet lined with paper toweling; sprinkle tops with paprika. Microwave, uncovered, at High power until hot, 3 to 6 minutes; rotate dish ½ turn after about half of cooking time. Sprinkle with remaining onion.

Makes 6 servings

Lemon-Zest Brussels Sprouts

1 pound (450 g) fresh
   Brussels sprouts, rinsed
¼ cup (60 mL) water
2 tablespoons (30 mL) butter
   or margarine
2 teaspoons (10 mL) lemon
   juice
½ teaspoon (2 mL) grated
   lemon rind
½ teaspoon (2 mL) salt
Pinch pepper
Pinch garlic powder

1. Trim and discard loose leaves and stems from Brussels sprouts. Cut a shallow cross in base of each sprout.

2. Combine sprouts and water in 1½-quart (1.5 L) casserole. Microwave, covered with lid, at High power just until crisp-tender, 4 to 8 minutes; stir twice during cooking. Let stand, covered, 3 minutes.

3. Microwave butter in small bowl, uncovered, at High power until melted, 30 to 45 seconds. Stir in remaining ingredients.

4. Drain Brussels sprouts. Add butter mixture to sprouts; stir to coat well.

Makes 4 to 6 servings

Eggplant Marinara Gratin

1 medium onion, chopped
½ cup (125 mL) chopped green bell pepper
1 small clove garlic, minced
1 tablespoon (15 mL) olive oil
½ cup (125 mL) tomato sauce
1 can (6 ounces or 170 g) tomato paste
2 tablespoons (30 mL) minced fresh parsley
1 teaspoon (5 mL) sugar
½ teaspoon (2 mL) dried basil, crumbled
¼ teaspoon (1 mL) dried oregano, crumbled
⅛ teaspoon (0.5 mL) dried hot red pepper flakes
1 medium eggplant (about 1¼ pounds or 565 g)
8 ounces (225 g) mozzarella cheese, shredded
3 tablespoons (45 mL) grated Parmesan cheese

1. Combine onion, green pepper and garlic in 2-quart (2 L) casserole. Add oil; stir. Microwave, uncovered, at High power until onion and pepper are tender, 2½ to 3 minutes.

2. Stir in tomato sauce and paste, parsley, sugar, basil, oregano and pepper flakes. Microwave, uncovered, at High power until sauce is bubbly, 3 to 5 minutes; stir once during cooking.

3. Cut eggplant into ½-inch (1.5 cm) cubes; place in 8×8-inch (20×20 cm) baking dish. Microwave, covered with waxed paper, at High power until tender, 6 to 8 minutes; stir once during cooking.

4. Sprinkle eggplant evenly with ½ the mozzarella and Parmesan cheeses. Spread sauce mixture evenly over cheese. Top evenly with remaining cheeses.

5. Microwave, uncovered, at High power until cheese melts, 3 to 5 minutes; rotate dish ½ turn after about half of cooking time.

Makes 4 servings

Spiced Baby Carrots

12 ounces (340 g) fresh baby carrots, pared or scrubbed*
2 tablespoons (30 mL) water
3 tablespoons (45 mL) butter or margarine
3 tablespoons (45 mL) packed brown sugar
½ teaspoon (2 mL) ground nutmeg
¼ teaspoon (1 mL) salt
Pinch ground cinnamon
½ teaspoon (2 mL) grated orange rind
3 tablespoons (45 mL) chopped pecans, if desired

Frozen whole baby carrots can be substituted for fresh. Use 1 pound (450 g) frozen carrots; increase microwave time in Step 1 to 6½ to 8½ minutes.

1. Place carrots and water in 1-quart (1 L) casserole. Microwave, covered with lid, at High power just until crisp-tender, 6 to 8 minutes; stir once during cooking. Let carrots stand, covered, 3 minutes.

2. Microwave butter in 4-cup (1 L) measure, uncovered, at High power until melted, 30 to 45 seconds. Stir in sugar, nutmeg, salt and cinnamon.

3. Microwave sugar mixture, uncovered, at High power just until sugar is melted, 15 to 20 seconds; stir well. Drain carrots. Add sugar mixture; stir to coat well. Stir in orange rind. Transfer to serving dish; sprinkle with pecans.

Makes 4 servings

Cauliflower Toss

3 tablespoons (45 mL) soy
  sauce
1 teaspoon (5 mL)
  cornstarch
½ teaspoon (2 mL) minced
  pared fresh ginger root
¼ teaspoon (1 mL) sugar
4 cups (1 L) small
  cauliflower flowerets
2 cups (500 mL) sliced fresh
  mushrooms
⅓ cup (80 mL) chopped
  green onion
¼ cup (60 mL) slivered
  almonds
2 tablespoons (30 mL) butter
  or margarine

1. Combine soy sauce, cornstarch, ginger root and sugar in medium bowl; stir until smooth. Add cauliflower, mushrooms, onion, and almonds; stir to mix well. Marinate at room temperature 10 minutes.

2. Microwave butter in 2-quart (2 L) flat casserole, uncovered, at High power until melted, 30 to 45 seconds. Stir in reserved vegetable mixture.

3. Microwave, covered with lid, at High power until cauliflower is crisp-tender, 6 to 9 minutes; stir after about half of cooking time.

Makes 4 to 6 servings

Harvest Glow Squash

2 whole acorn squash
  (1½ pounds or 675 g
  each)
⅛ to ¼ teaspoon (0.5 to
  1 mL) ground nutmeg
2 teaspoons (10 mL) lemon
  juice
¼ cup (60 mL) butter or
  margarine
¼ cup (60 mL) packed
  brown sugar
¼ cup (60 mL) chopped
  pecans

1. To facilitate cutting, microwave squash at High power 1½ minutes. Cut each squash lengthwise in half; scoop out and discard seeds and fibers.

2. Cover cut surface of each squash half with plastic wrap. Arrange squash evenly spaced in microwave oven. Microwave at High power until squash is tender, 10 to 15 minutes; rearrange squash and rotate ½ turn after about half of cooking time.

3. Uncover squash. Sprinkle centers with nutmeg and drizzle with lemon juice, dividing evenly. Add 1 tablespoon (15 mL) each of the butter, sugar and pecans to center of each squash half. Cover with plastic wrap. Let stand 5 to 10 minutes before serving.

Makes 4 servings

Summer Garden Zucchini Boats

1 slice bacon
2 medium zucchini, scrubbed (about 1 pound or 450 g)
⅓ cup (80 mL) finely chopped Spanish or yellow onion
1 tablespoon (15 mL) olive oil
1 small clove garlic, minced
½ cup (125 mL) seeded, coarsely chopped fresh tomato
⅓ cup (80 mL) dry bread crumbs
1 tablespoon (15 mL) grated Parmesan cheese
¼ teaspoon (1 mL) dried oregano, crumbled
¼ teaspoon (1 mL) salt
Pinch cayenne pepper

1. Place bacon on double thickness of paper toweling; fold toweling over bacon to cover. Microwave at High power until slightly underdone, 45 to 60 seconds. Let stand, covered, 5 minutes to complete cooking. Crumble bacon.

2. Cut zucchini lengthwise in half. Scoop out centers of zucchini with spoon, leaving ¼-inch (0.5 cm) shells. Coarsely chop zucchini pulp.

3. Combine onion, oil and garlic in medium bowl. Microwave, uncovered, at High power until onion is tender, 1½ to 2½ minutes. Add tomato, bread crumbs, cheese, oregano, salt, pepper, bacon and zucchini pulp; mix well.

4. Spoon tomato mixture into zucchini shells, mounding slightly. Arrange evenly spaced in 12×8-inch (30×20 cm) baking dish.

5. Microwave stuffed zucchini, uncovered, at High power until shells are tender, 6 to 8 minutes; rotate dish ½ turn after about half of cooking time.

Makes 4 servings

Artichokes with Creamy Mustard Dip

4 whole fresh artichokes
4 teaspoons (20 mL) lemon juice
6 ounces (170 g) cream cheese
¼ cup (60 mL) mayonnaise
2 teaspoons (10 mL) Dijon-style mustard
½ teaspoon (2 mL) salt
¼ teaspoon (1 mL) minced garlic
Pinch white pepper
¼ teaspoon (1 mL) paprika

1. Cut 1 inch (2.5 cm) off top of each artichoke with sharp knife; cut off stems leaving base flat. Pull off small leaves at base of artichokes. Cut off sharp tips of outer leaves with scissors.

2. Rinse artichokes; shake off excess water. Quickly brush cut surfaces with 2 teaspoons (10 mL) of the lemon juice to prevent discoloration. Wrap each artichoke in plastic wrap.

3. Arrange artichokes, evenly spaced, in microwave. Microwave at High power until base can be easily pierced with fork and lower leaves can be pulled off with slight tug, 9½ to 14½ minutes; rearrange artichokes after about half of cooking time. Let stand, wrapped, 3 minutes.

4. Microwave cream cheese in medium bowl, uncovered, at High power until softened, 20 to 30 seconds. Beat cream cheese with wooden spoon until smooth; beat in mayonnaise. Add remaining 2 teaspoons (10 mL) lemon juice, mustard, salt, garlic and pepper; stir to mix well. Transfer dip to 4 individual small serving bowls. Sprinkle tops with paprika. Serve with artichokes.

Makes 4 servings

Viva Tomatoes

4 medium tomatoes
2 cups (500 mL) coarsely
    chopped mushrooms
⅓ cup (80 mL) chopped
    celery
¼ cup (60 mL) chopped
    onion
3 tablespoons (45 mL) butter
    or margarine
⅓ cup (80 mL) dry bread
    crumbs
¼ teaspoon (1 mL) garlic
    salt
⅛ teaspoon (0.5 mL) dried
    thyme
1 large egg, lightly beaten
¾ cup (180 mL) shredded
    Cheddar cheese

1. Slice off tops of tomatoes; scoop out seeds and pulp. Place tomatoes in 8×8-inch (20×20 cm) baking dish.

2. Place mushrooms, celery, onion and butter in 1-quart (1

L) casserole; stir to mix. Microwave, uncovered, at High power until celery is crisp-tender, 3½ to 4½ minutes; stir twice during cooking.

3. Add bread crumbs, garlic salt, thyme, egg and ½ cup (125 mL) cheese to casserole; stir until well blended and cheese is melted. Spoon mixture into tomatoes, dividing evenly.

4. Microwave tomatoes, covered with plastic wrap, at High power until tomatoes are tender, 3½ to 4½ minutes; rotate dish ½ turn after about half of cooking time.

5. Sprinkle remaining ¼ cup (60 mL) cheese over tops of tomatoes, dividing evenly. Let stand, covered with plastic wrap, until cheese melts, 1 to 2 minutes.

Making 2 to 4 servings

Herb-Buttered Corn

4 or 5 fresh ears corn (about
    8 ounces or 225 g each),
    husked
¼ cup (60 mL) water
½ cup (125 mL) butter or
    margarine
½ teaspoon (2 mL) finely
    chopped fresh or dried
    chives
¼ teaspoon (1 mL) salt
⅛ teaspoon (0.5 mL) pepper
1 tablespoon (15 mL) grated
    Parmesan cheese, if
    desired

1. Place corn in 13×9-inch (33×23 cm) baking dish; leave space between ears. Add the water to dish.*

2. Microwave, covered with plastic wrap, at High power until tender, 8 to 15 minutes; turn ears and rearrange every 4 minutes. Let stand, covered, 5 minutes.

3. Combine butter, chives, salt and pepper in small bowl. Microwave, uncovered, at High power until butter melts, 1½ to 2½ minutes; stir once during cooking. Stir in cheese. Pour over corn.

Makes 4 or 5 servings

Ears of corn may be individually wrapped in plastic wrap, without water. Place directly on oven floor, leaving space between ears. Microwave as in Step 2.

Apple Crumb Pie

CRUMB PASTRY
2 cups (500 mL) all-purpose
  flour
1 teaspoon (5 mL) salt
⅔ cup (160 mL) shortening
3 tablespoons (45 mL) butter
  or margarine
¼ cup (60 mL) cold water

APPLE FILLING
4 to 5 cups (1 to 1.25 L)
  sliced pared apples
⅔ cup (160 mL) sugar
½ teaspoon (2 mL) ground
  cinnamon
2 tablespoons (30 mL) all-
  purpose flour

1. For Pastry: Mix flour and salt in large bowl. Cut in shortening and butter with pastry blender until mixture resembles coarse crumbs.

2. Transfer 1½ cups (375 mL) mixture to a pie plate. Sprinkle 2 tablespoons (30 mL) water over mixture in plate, tossing with fork until well mixed, but crumbly;

spread evenly in plate. Microwave, uncovered, at High power 5 minutes. Cool; crumble finely and reserve.

3. While stirring with fork, sprinkle enough of remaining water over mixture in bowl, just until moist enough to form a ball. Roll out pastry on floured surface to ⅛-inch (0.5 cm) thick circle about 2 inches larger than inverted pie plate.

Fold pastry into quarters; then unfold and fit gently and carefully into clean pie plate. (Do not stretch pastry.)

4. Let pastry rest 10 minutes. Trim overhang to generous ½ inch (1.5 cm); fold under to form standing rim. Place left index finger inside rim and right thumb and index finger on outside of rim; push pastry into "V" shape every ½ inch (1.5 cm) around plate. Pinch flutes to make sharp edges.

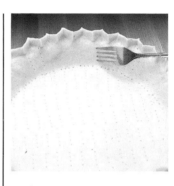

5. Prick crust continuously with fork at bend of plate and make pricks ½ inch (1.5 cm) apart on side and all across bottom. Microwave, uncovered, at High power until bottom appears dry, 4 to 7 minutes; rotate ¼ or ½ turn every 1 to 3 minutes as needed to cook crust evenly (watch closely).

6. For Filling: Combine filling ingredients in large bowl; stir to coat apples evenly. Microwave, uncovered, at High power just until apples are tender, about 5 minutes; stir once during cooking.

7. Spread apples in crust. Sprinkle with reserved crumbs. Set pie on waxed paper in microwave oven. Microwave, uncovered, at High power until filling is bubbly, 7 to 8 minutes; rotate pie ½ turn twice during cooking.

**Makes 9- or 10-inch
(23 or 25 cm) pie**

Strawberry Cheesecake

3 tablespoons (45 mL) butter
  or margarine
1 cup (250 mL) graham
  cracker crumbs
¾ cup (180 mL) plus
  2 tablespoons (30 mL)
  sugar
2 packages (8 ounces or
  225 g each) cream cheese
⅓ cup (80 mL) sour cream
¼ teaspoon (1 mL) salt
4 large eggs
3 tablespoons (45 mL)
  lemon juice
2 teaspoons (10 mL) grated
  lemon rind
¼ teaspoon (1 mL) vanilla
1 package (10 ounces or
  285 g) frozen sweetened
  strawberries
1 tablespoon (15 mL)
  cornstarch

1. Microwave butter in 9-inch (23 cm) round baking dish, uncovered, at High power until melted, 30 to 45 seconds. Add crumbs, stirring and tossing with fork until evenly moistened. Stir in 2 tablespoons (30 mL) sugar.

2. Spread crumb mixture in even layer in dish; press firmly with fingers. Microwave, uncovered, at High power 1½ minutes; rotate dish ½ turn after 1 minute of cooking.

3. Microwave cream cheese in large bowl, uncovered, at Medium (50%) power until softened, about 1 minute. Beat until smooth. Beat in the remaining ¾ cup (180 mL) sugar, the sour cream and salt. Add eggs one at a time, beating well on medium speed after each addition.

Stir in 2 tablespoons (30 mL) lemon juice, the lemon rind and vanilla.

4. Microwave cheese mixture, uncovered, at High power just until very hot, 3 to 5 minutes; stir every 2 minutes. Pour mixture over crumb mixture; spread top smooth.

5. Microwave cheesecake, uncovered, at Medium (50%) power until filling is almost set in center, 7 to 12 minutes; rotate dish ¼ turn every 3 minutes during cooking. (Filling will firm up as cake cools.) Cool completely on wire rack. Refrigerate, covered, at least 8 hours or overnight.

6. For Topping: Microwave strawberries in package on paper plate at High power just until soft, 1 to 3 minutes; berries will be slightly icy. (If package has metal ends, run under hot water briefly and transfer berries from package to small bowl before microwaving.)

7. Drain juice from strawberries into small bowl. Stir in cornstarch until dissolved. Stir in strawberries. Microwave, uncovered, at High power until thickened and clear, 2 to 5 minutes; stir mixture after each minute of cooking. Stir in remaining 1 tablespoon (15 mL) lemon juice. Cool completely. Serve with cheesecake or spoon over cake before serving.

Makes 8 to 10 servings

Fabulous Fudge

2 cups (500 mL) sugar
5 tablespoons (75 mL)
  unsweetened cocoa
  powder
¼ teaspoon (1 mL) salt
1 cup (250 mL) evaporated
  milk
1½ tablespoons (22 mL)
  light corn syrup
4 tablespoons (60 mL) butter
  or margarine
1 teaspoon (5 mL) vanilla
½ cup (125 mL) chopped
  nuts, if desired

1. Combine sugar, cocoa and salt in 3- to 3½-quart (3 to 3.5 L) casserole. Stir in milk and corn syrup; mix well. Cut 3 tablespoons (45 mL) of the butter into 3 pieces; add to casserole.

2. Microwave, covered, at High power 5 minutes. Stir to mix well. Microwave, uncovered, at High power until mixture reaches soft-ball stage, 10 to 12 minutes. Test by spooning a small amount of mixture into ice water; it should form a soft ball.

3. Cool mixture, without stirring, to lukewarm. (After 10 minutes, casserole can be placed in shallow bowl of cool water to hasten cooling, if desired.)

4. Spread remaining 1 tablespoon (15 mL) butter on bottom and sides of 10×6-inch (25×15 cm) loaf dish. Reserve.

5. Stir vanilla and nuts into cooled mixture; beat until fudge becomes thick and begins to lose its gloss and hold its shape. Quickly transfer fudge to prepared dish; spread evenly. Cut into squares when firm.

Makes about 1 pound

Oatmeal Date Bars

DATE FILLING
- 1¼ cups (310 mL) dates, chopped
- 7 tablespoons (105 mL) water
- 2 tablespoons (30 mL) granulated sugar
- 1 tablespoon (15 mL) lemon juice

BASE
- 1 cup (250 mL) quick-cooking oats
- 1 cup (250 mL) all-purpose flour
- ⅔ cup (160 mL) packed light brown sugar
- ½ teaspoon (2 mL) ground cinnamon, if desired
- ¼ teaspoon (1 mL) salt
- ¼ teaspoon (1 mL) baking soda
- ½ cup (125 mL) butter or margarine

1. For Filling: Combine dates, water, granulated sugar and lemon juice in medium bowl. Microwave, uncovered, at High power until thick and smooth, 3 to 5 minutes; stir after each minute of cooking. Reserve filling.

2. For Base: Mix oats, flour, brown sugar, cinnamon, salt and soda in large bowl. Cut in butter with pastry blender until mixture resembles coarse crumbs. Reserve 1 cup (250 mL) oatmeal mixture. Press remaining oatmeal mixture firmly and evenly in 8×8-inch (20×20 cm) baking dish to form base of bars.

3. Place inverted saucer in microwave oven; center baking dish on saucer. Microwave oatmeal base, uncovered, at Medium (50%) power until base appears dry, 3 to 7 minutes; rotate dish ¼ turn every 2 minutes during cooking.

4. Spoon date filling over oatmeal base; spread carefully into even layer. Sprinkle evenly with reserved 1 cup (250 mL) oatmeal mixture. Microwave, uncovered, at High power until oatmeal topping is dry and cooked through, 4 to 8 minutes; rotate dish ½ turn every 2 minutes during cooking. Cool completely. Cut into bars.

Makes about 16 bars

Fresh Fruit Compote

- 2 medium ripe peaches
- 1 large ripe pear
- 1 cup (250 mL) fresh sweet cherries
- 1 cup (250 mL) fresh or drained canned pineapple chunks
- ¼ cup (60 mL) water
- 1 tablespoon (15 mL) kirsch
- ¾ cup (180 mL) packed brown sugar

1. Peel and pit peaches. Core pear. Cut peaches and pear lengthwise into ½-inch (1.5 cm) thick slices. Pit cherries, if desired.

2. Combine peaches, pear, cherries, pineapple and water in 2-quart (2 L) casserole. Microwave, covered with lid, at High power until fruit is almost tender throughout but not soft, 5 to 8 minutes; stir mixture after first 4 minutes of cooking.

3. Add kirsch and sugar to fruit; mix well. Cover casserole with lid; let fruit mixture stand 2 minutes. Serve warm, at room temperature or cold.

Makes 4 to 6 servings.

Chocolate-Dream Cake

¼ cup (60 mL) butter or margarine
1 cup (250 mL) graham cracker crumbs
½ cup (125 mL) chopped walnuts
6 ounces (170 g) semisweet chocolate
1¾ cups (430 mL) all-purpose flour
1¼ cups (310 mL) granulated sugar
1 teaspoon (5 mL) baking soda
1 teaspoon (5 mL) salt
4 large eggs
¾ cup (180 mL) buttermilk
⅔ cup (160 mL) plus 1 tablespoon (15 mL) solid vegetable shortening
2 teaspoons (10 mL) vanilla
1½ cups (375 mL) whipping cream
3 tablespoons (45 mL) powdered sugar

1. Microwave butter in small bowl, uncovered, at High power until melted, 45 to 60 seconds. Add crumbs; stir and toss until evenly moistened. Microwave at High power 1 minute, stirring once. Stir in nuts; reserve topping.

2. Line bottoms of two 9-inch (23 cm) round cake dishes with waxed-paper circles.

3. Microwave 2 ounces (60 g) of the chocolate in small bowl, uncovered, at Medium (50%) power, stirring occasionally, until melted and smooth, 2 to 4 minutes.

4. Mix flour, granulated sugar, baking soda and salt in large mixer bowl. Add eggs, buttermilk, ⅔ cup (160 mL) of the shortening and 1 teaspoon (5 mL) of the vanilla; beat at low speed, scraping bowl constantly, just until blended. Beat batter at medium speed, scraping occasionally, 2 minutes. Stir melted chocolate; add to batter. Beat just until evenly blended.

5. Pour batter into cake dishes, dividing evenly. Microwave 1 layer at a time as follows: Microwave, uncovered, at Medium (50%) power 5 minutes; rotate ¼ turn after 3 minutes. Sprinkle with ½ the reserved topping. Microwave, uncovered, at High power until center springs back when lightly pressed, 1 to 4 minutes; rotate ¼ turn twice during cooking. Let cake stand directly on heat-proof counter, uncovered, 10 minutes. Repeat with second layer. Remove layers from dishes; cool completely on wire racks.

6. Combine remaining 4 ounces (115 g) chocolate and 1 tablespoon (15 mL) shortening in 2-cup (500 mL) measure. Microwave, uncovered, at Medium (50%) power until chocolate is soft and shiny, 2½ to 5½ minutes. Stir until smooth; drizzle over cake layers in criss-cross pattern, dividing evenly. Let stand until chocolate sets.

7. Combine cream, powdered sugar and remaining 1 teaspoon (5 mL) vanilla in medium bowl; beat until stiff. Spoon about ⅔ of the whipped cream on one cake layer on serving plate; spread evenly. Top with second layer. Press remaining whipped cream through pastry bag fitted with star tip in border on top of cake. Refrigerate cake until serving time.

Makes 10 servings

Lemon & Cream Pie

CRUST
5 tablespoons (75 mL) butter
or margarine
1⅓ cups (330 mL) fine
graham cracker crumbs
2 tablespoons (30 mL) sugar

FILLING
1 cup (250 mL) sugar
¼ cup (60 mL) cornstarch
¼ teaspoon (1 mL) salt
1¾ cups (430 mL) water
3 large egg yolks, lightly
beaten
2 tablespoons (30 mL) butter
or margarine, at room
temperature
⅓ cup (80 mL) fresh lemon
juice
1 tablespoon (15 mL) grated
lemon rind

TOPPING
1½ cups (375 mL) whipping
cream

1. For Crust: Microwave butter in 9-inch (23 cm) pie plate, uncovered, at High power until melted, 45 to 60 seconds. Add crumbs and sugar; stir and toss until crumbs are evenly moistened.

2. Spread crumb mixture evenly on bottom and sides of pie plate; press crumbs firmly against plate with bottom of custard cup or glass. Microwave, uncovered, at High power 1½ minutes; rotate plate ½ turn after 1 minute of cooking. Cool, uncovered, on wire rack.

3. For Filling: Combine sugar, cornstarch and salt in 1½-quart (1.5 L) casserole. Add ½ cup (125 mL) of the water; stir until cornstarch is dissolved.

4. Microwave remaining 1¼ cups (310 mL) water in 2-cup (500 mL) measure, uncovered, at High power until boiling, 2 to 3 minutes. Gradually stir into sugar mixture. Microwave sugar mixture, uncovered, at High power until very thick, 4 to 6 minutes; stir every 2 minutes during cooking.

5. Gradually stir about ¼ of the hot mixture into egg yolks in small bowl. Gradually stir egg yolk mixture into remaining hot mixture in casserole. Microwave, uncovered, at High power 1 minute. Add butter; stir until melted. Stir in lemon juice and rind. Cool filling 10 minutes. Pour filling into crumb crust; cool completely.

6. Before serving, beat cream in large mixer bowl until stiff; spread over top of pie.

Makes 9-inch (23 cm) pie

Brandy-Fudge Sundaes

1 cup (250 mL) sugar
¼ cup (60 mL) unsweetened
cocoa powder
1 tablespoon (15 mL) all-
purpose flour
½ cup (125 mL) milk
2 tablespoons (30 mL) light
corn syrup
2 tablespoons (30 mL) butter
or margarine
½ teaspoon (2 mL) vanilla
2 teaspoons (10 mL) brandy
Vanilla ice cream

1. Combine sugar, cocoa and flour in 4-cup (1 L) measure or in 1½-quart (1.5 L) bowl. Stir until flour and cocoa are evenly dispersed in sugar with no lumps remaining. Gradually pour in milk, stirring until smooth. Stir in corn syrup; add butter.

2. Microwave mixture, uncovered, at High power until thick, smooth and a rich chocolate color, 4 to 8 minutes; stir every 2 minutes during cooking.

3. Stir vanilla and brandy into sauce; mix well. Serve about ¼ cup (60 mL) warm sauce over scoops of vanilla ice cream.*

Makes about 6 servings

Leftover sauce can be stored, covered, in refrigerator. To reheat: Microwave, covered with plastic wrap, at High power just until heated through, 15 to 30 seconds for each ½ cup (125 mL) sauce.

Variations: For Coffee-Fudge Sundaes, add 1 teaspoon (15 mL) instant coffee powder with the cocoa; omit brandy. For plain Hot Fudge Sundaes, add ⅛ teaspoon (0.5 mL) salt with the cocoa; omit brandy.

Ambrosia Cake

1 package (18½ ounces or
   525 g) yellow cake mix
2 cans (8¼ ounces or 232 g
   each) crushed pineapple,
   undrained
3 large eggs
⅓ cup (80 mL) vegetable oil
2 cups (500 mL) shredded
   coconut
¼ cup (60 mL) butter or
   margarine
4 cups (1 L) powdered sugar
2 to 3 tablespoons (30 to
   45 mL) rum or half-and-
   half
1 teaspoon (5 mL) vanilla

1. Line bottom and sides of 8×8-inch (20×20 cm) cake dish with 2 sheets of waxed paper, leaving 1-inch (2.5 cm) overhang on all sides. Repeat with second cake dish.

2. Combine cake mix, pineapple, eggs and oil in large mixer bowl. Beat at low speed, scraping bowl constantly, until ingredients are blended. Beat at medium speed, scraping occasionally, 2 minutes. Stir in 1 cup (250 mL) of the coconut. Pour batter into cake dishes, dividing evenly.

3. Microwave 1 cake at a time as follows: Place cake dish in oven on inverted saucer. Microwave, uncovered, at Medium (50%) power 6 minutes; rotate ½ turn after 4

minutes of cooking. Microwave, uncovered, at High power until center springs back when lightly pressed and no unbaked batter is visible through bottom of dish, 3 to 6 minutes. Let stand directly on heatproof counter, uncovered, 10 minutes; then place dish on wire rack to cool completely. Repeat with second layer.

4. Spread remaining 1 cup (250 mL) coconut on paper plate. Microwave, uncovered, at High power, stirring 2 or 3 times, until toasted, 1½ to 3 minutes.

5. Microwave butter in medium bowl, uncovered, at Medium (50%) power until softened, 10 to 15 seconds. Add 2 cups (500 mL) of the sugar, 2 tablespoons (30 mL) of the rum and the vanilla; beat until smooth. Gradually beat in the remaining sugar. Beat in as much of the remaining rum, a few drops at a time, as needed to make smooth spreadable frosting.

6. Spread frosting on tops of cakes, dividing evenly. Sprinkle each cake with ½ the toasted coconut. Loosen cakes by gently pulling up on waxed paper overhang; lift from dish.* Slide cakes onto serving plates, removing waxed paper.

Makes 2 single-layer cakes

If desired, freeze 1 cake on wire rack until firm; wrap tightly and freeze up to 1 month. To thaw: Unwrap cake and place on plate. Microwave, uncovered, at Medium-Low (30%) power until wooden pick can be inserted easily into center and frosting is softened but not melted, 5 to 8 minutes; rotate plate ¼ turn every minute. Let stand, uncovered, 10 minutes.

Coconut-Cream Dessert Dip

⅓ cup (80 mL) shredded
  coconut
1 cup (250 mL)
  marshmallow cream
2 to 3 tablespoons (30 to
  45 mL) red raspberry
  preserves
1 cup (250 mL) sour cream
¼ cup (60 mL) chopped
  walnuts
Mint leaves, if desired
Fruit for dipping (whole
  strawberries, green
  grapes, cantaloupe balls,
  honeydew melon balls,
  watermelon balls,
  nectarine slices)

1. Spread coconut in 9-inch (23 cm) pie plate. Microwave, uncovered, at Medium-High (70%) power until light brown, 3 to 4 minutes; toss with fork after each minute. Cool.

2. Microwave marshmallow cream in medium bowl, uncovered, at Medium-High (70%) power until softened, about 1 minute. Stir in preserves until smooth. [If mixture is not smooth, microwave at Medium-High (70%) power about 30 seconds longer; stir until smooth.] Stir in toasted coconut.

3. Add sour cream and walnuts; mix well. Spoon into serving bowl. Cover; refrigerate until chilled. Garnish with mint leaves. Serve with fresh fruit for dipping.

Makes about 2 cups

Favorite Brownies

½ cup (125 mL) butter or
  margarine, cut into 4
  pieces
6 tablespoons (90 mL)
  unsweetened cocoa
  powder
¾ cup (180 mL) sugar
2 large eggs
2 tablespoons (30 mL) milk
1 teaspoon (5 mL) vanilla
⅔ cup (160 mL) all-purpose
  flour
½ teaspoon (2 mL) baking
  powder
¼ teaspoon (1 mL) salt
½ cup (125 mL) chopped
  pecans or walnuts

1. Place butter and cocoa in 8×8-inch (20×20 cm) baking dish. Microwave, uncovered, at High power until butter is melted, 1 to 1½ minutes.

2. Add sugar to baking dish; stir to mix well. Add remaining ingredients; mix well, especially in corners. Spread batter evenly in dish.

3. Shield 4 corners of baking dish with aluminum foil triangles to prevent overcooking in corners.

4. Microwave, uncovered, at High power until top is no longer wet, 5 to 6 minutes; rotate dish ½ turn after 3 minutes.

5. Place baking dish directly on heatproof counter; let stand 10 minutes to complete cooking. Cut brownies into 2-inch (5 cm) squares.

Makes 16 brownies

Ice Cream Tunnel Cake

Shortening
2 tablespoons (30 mL) sugar
1 package (2 layer size) chocolate cake mix
Eggs
Water
1 quart (1 L) vanilla ice cream
½ cup (125 mL) mint-flavored semisweet chocolate morsels
½ cup (125 mL) light corn syrup
1 tablespoon (15 mL) light cream or half-and-half
½ teaspoon (2 mL) vanilla

1. Grease 12- to 14-cup (3 to 3.5 L) ring cake dish with shortening. Sprinkle dish with sugar; shake and rotate to coat evenly and tap out excess. Prepare cake mix with eggs and water according to package directions; pour batter into cake dish and spread evenly.

2. Microwave cake, uncovered, at Medium (50%) power 12 minutes; rotate dish

¼ turn every 4 minutes. Then microwave at High power until cake begins to pull away from sides of dish, 4 to 7 minutes. Let stand 10 minutes. Carefully loosen inner and outer edges of cake; unmold onto wire rack. Cool completely.

3. Slice off top ¼ of cake with serrated knife; reserve. With thin-bladed knife, cut around inner edge of cake, starting about ¾ inch (2 cm) in from edge and cutting to within 1 inch (2.5 cm) of bottom. Repeat, cutting around outer edge of cake.

4. Carefully scoop out center, cut portion of cake with spoon, leaving 1 inch (2.5 cm) of cake on bottom. Place cake shell in freezer for 1 hour. (Save cake center for other use.)

5. Place ice cream in medium bowl. Microwave, uncovered, at Medium-Low (30%) power just until softened, 30 to 60 seconds. Stir ice cream until smooth; spoon into cake shell. Cover with reserved cake top. Freeze, covered, at least 6 hours.

6. Before serving, combine chocolate morsels and corn syrup in medium bowl. Microwave, covered with plastic wrap, at High power until morsels are shiny and soft, 30 to 60 seconds. Stir until smooth. Stir in cream and vanilla. Spoon glaze over top of cake.

Makes 8 to 10 servings

Coffee-Rum Variation: Brush all cut surfaces of cake with 2 tablespoons (30 mL) rum; fill cake with coffee ice cream.

Caramel Turtlettes

5 dozen large pecan or walnut halves
1 teaspoon (5 mL) butter or margarine
2 dozen caramel candy cubes
1 cup (250 mL) semisweet chocolate morsels
2 tablespoons (30 mL) solid vegetable shortening

1. Cut 4 dozen of the pecan halves lengthwise in half. Cut the remaining 1 dozen pecan halves crosswise in half. For each turtle shape, arrange 4 long pecan pieces for the legs and 1 short piece for the head on waxed paper. Spread butter in bottom of pie plate to coat evenly.

2. Arrange 6 of the caramels in large circle in pie plate. Microwave, uncovered, at High power until caramels are soft but not melted on bottom, 15 to 30 seconds. Cover pie plate with sheet of waxed paper to keep caramels warm.

3. Place 1 warm caramel in center of a nut cluster; press down firmly and spread with fingers to attach pecan legs and head to caramel body. (If caramels become too hard to spread, microwave at High power 5 to 10 seconds to resoften.)

4. Repeat Steps 2 and 3, using 6 caramels at a time, to make a total of 24 turtlettes.

5. Combine chocolate morsels and shortening in small bowl. Microwave, covered with plastic wrap, at Medium

(50%) power until most of the morsels are shiny and soft, 4 to 6 minutes. Stir until smooth.

6. Hold each turtle by the head and dip into melted chocolate to coat both sides; shake off excess. Let stand on waxed paper at room temperature until chocolate is set.*

Makes 2 dozen

Chocolate coating can be used to coat pretzels, small cookies or large nuts.

Index